General Introduction

This piece was originally [illegible] ıatic readings for public perfor[illegible] ·iter through his own words an[illegible] o an audience which knew very [illegible] or his age, but might expect to meet either [illegible] in examination syllabuses or in a non-specialist English course. It was hoped this kind of dramatic presentation would give some idea of the preoccupations of the writer and the atmosphere of his time, and encourage further reading.

The original readings lasted about seventy minutes, but in book form they have been expanded, mainly with the sort of meat that a theatre audience cannot digest too much of. But some sauce remains in order that the readings may be as entertaining as possible.

The book is designed for anyone of fifteen or more who is approaching a writer or an age for the first time. Study of the classical English writers requires an imaginative leap. Language, style or form may initially make it hard for the student to see the writer as a person like himself, with the same problems and attitudes. He may imagine him as humourless, dry and dated, and his age as the more dated the further it is away. The idea, for example, that 17th and 18th-century figures are mostly livelier, funnier, cleverer and more knowledgeable than their counterparts in the 20th century may not occur to him. Nor may it seem obvious that we have progressed since 1700 only in a limited sense. If this series manages to put flesh on the dry bones of the past, it will have succeeded.

The book may be read out of school or, perhaps more usefully, aloud in the classroom with the parts distributed. In book form it is, of course, much too long to be read at a sitting. Short sections should be followed by discussion.

It is hoped that this series will also be valuable to the general reader who wants either simply to refresh his memory, or to explore a writer for the first time and needs an easy and brief introduction before setting forth.

An introduction precedes the text: it attempts to set each writer in perspective and to make an evaluation of his work.

Acknowledgment

The publisher's thanks are due to the Society of Authors on behalf of the Bernard Shaw Estate for permission to quote from the writings of G. B. Shaw.

The Portrait Series
General Editor: Tommy Cookson

SHAW

edited by Tommy Cookson

illustrated by George Gillespie

Edward Arnold

First published 1972
by Edward Arnold (Publishers) Ltd.,
41 Maddox Street,
London, W1R 0AN

ISBN: 0 7131 1708 7

Printed in Great Britain by
Billing & Sons Limited,
Guildford and London

Introduction

Bernard Shaw was born of Protestant stock in Dublin in 1856. He came to England in 1876 and, after spending a short time in casual employment, settled down to write novels. He wrote five, not one of which was accepted for publication. By 1880 he had become interested in politics and four years later he joined the Fabian Society, which brought him in touch with the advanced political thought of the day as well as some of the leading personalities. From this time his reputation as a speaker and socialist propagandist dates. He made a reputation as a writer with his music and dramatic criticism in *The Star and The World* (1888–1894). Finally the artist and propagandist in Shaw, guided by the example of the contemporary Norwegian playwright Henrik Ibsen, inevitably led him to write for the theatre: as he put it, "to substitute the Theatre for the Platform". His career as a playwright dates from the first performance of *Widowers' Houses* in 1892 which, though not rapturously received, was sufficiently promising to encourage further theatrical experiments culminating in the success of *Arms and the Man* in 1894. Shaw's reputation as a playwright was not, however, established in England until the early years of the 20th century when the Vedrenne-Granville Barker Management at the Royal Court Theatre at last brought him consistently before the London public. It was in New York that Richard Mansfield's production of the *Devil's Disciple* first made Shaw famous and comparatively wealthy. The two loathed one another and the collaboration was not long-lasting. Shaw's biographer Hesketh Pearson related that when Mansfield was told that he ought to go down on his knees and thank God for such a play, he replied that he did, but added "Why, O God, did it have to be by Shaw?".

By 1905 Shaw had become an established playwright and he continued to write plays until the end of his life. His plays are, as one would expect, very often about social and political problems and much of the dialogue is cast in the form of lively discussion between the characters. Initially his contemporaries found this tedious and undramatic, as if everybody talked and nobody did anything. *The Times* critic wrote, after seeing *Androcles and the*

Lion: "Of course it is the lion's evening. Was ever beast so fortunate? We do not mean in getting the thorn pulled out of his paw by Androcles; we mean in being the one character in the whole range of Shavian drama who never talks". "His propaganda – I beg pardon, his new play", apologised the *Penny Illustrated Paper*. But soon people began to think differently – Shaw's plays wore remarkably well. Far from being tedious, they proved to be very good theatre. Shaw himself was not slow to point out why: "The Devil's Disciple has, in truth, a genuine novelty in it. Only, that novelty is not any invention of my own, but simply the novelty of the advanced thought of my day. As such, it will assuredly lose its gloss with the lapse of time and leave *The Devil's Disciple* exposed as the threadbare popular melodrama it technically is".

"The threadbare popular melodrama it technically is." Well, perhaps Shaw, for once in a way, is being unduly modest. Yet he was to claim repeatedly that his plays represented nothing new from the technical point of view. "A frightful bag of old stage tricks" he was to call *The Apple Cart* (1928); "I found the surest way to produce the effect of daring innovation and originality was to revive the ancient attraction of long speeches; to stick closely to the methods of Molière; and to lift characters bodily out of the pages of Charles Dickens". Shaw's secret then was simply to combine the old conventions with "the advanced thought of my day".

Perhaps. Perhaps not. In any case Shaw attached great importance to the play of ideas – "and the drama can never be anything more". There can be no new drama without a new philosophy". He saw the theatre as a platform for his ideas and the drama as a socially influential force. Ibsen, he said, was a great playwright because *A Doll's House* would do good work in the world. Shakespeare was merely an observer. Ibsen (and Shaw) were thinkers.

Shaw's ideas spanned a number of topics: *Widowers' Houses* (slum landlords and the iniquity of the rich living off the extortionate rents of the poor): *Arms and the Man* (a spoof on the army and military glory): *Caesar and Cleopatra*, 1897, (an essay in political strategy): *Man and Superman*, 1902, (a vision of the New Society with a definition of Heaven): *John Bull's Other Island*, 1904, (Ireland): *Major Barbara*, 1950, (The Salvation Army and the problem of poverty): *The Doctor's Dilemma*, 1906, (an indirect plea for a National Health Scheme): *Getting Married*, 1908, (marriage). Throughout his plays can be traced a plea for the equality of the sexes – a perennial plank of the Socialist platform – and incidentally a reason why Shaw's women are the liveliest and most independent since Shakespeare's.

Yet few of Shaw's plays are directly about political and social problems: they have a life of their own which often leads Shaw the artist away from Shaw the politician. Raymond Williams has written in a readable and provocative essay: "Shaw is able to tell us, by naming a problem, what each of his plays is about; and the phrase is always an adequate explanation". This is a misleading remark, if it suggests that Shaw writes abstract discussions in which his characters do not emerge as personalities. They do. They pull the problem all over the place so that the audience frequently feels that the problem may have been the springboard of a play in which it is not even remotely answered. "When I start a play," said Shaw, "I have no idea what is going to happen." The winner of a Shavian discussion is not necessarily a supporter of the idea propounded in the Preface of the Play – he may possess simply more vitality than the person with the correct ideology. Shaw the artist frequently turns his back on Shaw the politician.

Inevitably, it seems to me, Shaw gravitated towards religion. Socialism is a kind of religion, except that it seeks to establish the Kingdom of God on earth by making all men equal in fact as well as in theory. Yet Shaw was too much of a realist not to see the limitation of socialism in practice, and too much of an idealist to accept it as a compromise. No 'ism' would ever have done for Shaw, who was too interested in human beings and who, in a curious way, was rather a romantic. It has been said that Shaw did not understand human feelings (Raymond Williams, in the essay quoted above, attacks such a personal play as *Candida* (1895) as 'inflated sentimentality') but it is clear that Shaw understood the religious impulse from experience of it and it is no accident that his most profound and successful plays (*Major Barbara*, 1905; *Androcles and the Lion*, 1913; and *St. Joan*, 1923) deal with religious topics. Shaw may indeed with justice be called a religious man rather than a socialist (Winston Churchill in his book *Great Contemporaries* wittily points out how Shaw's practice so frequently contradicted what he preached – not least in the matter of Socialist principles). He was not committed to Socialism in the way that, all his life, he seems to have been committed to the attainment of an ideal of happiness which went beyond anything that Socialism could achieve. What he saw in Socialism was a means to an end. By providing every man with a decent income, employment and accommodation, Socialism freed a man to concentrate on more important things and made him a responsible being. The worst thing in life, said Shaw, was to be used by personally-minded men for purposes which you recognise to be base. The best thing, on the other hand, was to be fired with a moral idea – not until then did a man realise his full potential. And nobody could do this unless his animal needs had been taken care of.

Since he felt the necessity for man to be responsible, Shaw concentrated his attack on two sorts of belief. The first was the belief in an omnipotent God. If God is omnipotent, he argued, then all responsibility is taken out of our hands and our sole function is to worship and obey. But when we look around us and see all sorts of evil and suffering which continue in spite of our prayers, such worship is horrible. "It is the stronger spirits, the thinkers, those with a high ideal of God and the power and courage to criticise and judge God by the standard of that high ideal, who revolt against his cruelty, denouncing him as the Almighty Fiend of Shelley; and finally rejecting the tale of his existence as a hideous dream. Although atheism may be mere stupidity, yet the intelligent atheist is generally superior to the average worshipper in intellect and in character as well." It therefore becomes necessary to believe in a God who did indeed create us as best he could, but left it to us to carry on where he left off. We are the instrument that God has chosen to perfect the world he made.

The second belief Shaw attacked was the Darwinist theory of Natural Selection: the fittest survive and the weaker go to the wall. It was a belief that left morality out of account; it justified anyone's doing anything. To Shaw the First World War was "sound Neo-Darwinism". In the name of a patriotic British God Germany was kicked to death after she had been knocked down. The Darwinist Theory, however, was only the chief target in Shaw's campaign against the March of Science. Technological progress without moral progress could threaten our whole civilisation. Furthermore, the belief of man in progress for progress's sake made him sanction such cruelties as vivisection. But did the end justify the means?

It is this moral intensity that accounts for Shaw's stature as a critic. His music and theatre criticism is passionate, forceful – and often wildly funny. He writes about art as if it mattered: "the true critic," he said, "is a man who becomes your personal enemy on the sole provocation of a bad performance." The extracts from his criticism quoted in this book seem primarily to condemn insincerity in art, i.e. giving the public what the public wants, not what the writer thinks the public should be given. From this lack of sincerity proceeds lack of energy and intensity. The playwright *must* treat his characters and situations as if they were real – not make theatrical short-cuts; the composer of oratorio must compose music which is suited to the words – not fit them to the musical style he finds easiest. Shaw regards the music in Parry's *Job* as decorative – it does not try to translate words into their musical equivalent, as Wagner translates the German myths. Parry refuses to commit himself whole-heartedly to the spirit of the words. As Shaw says: "Art has never been great when it was not providing an iconography for a live religion. And it has never been quite contemptible except when imitating the iconography after the religion had become a superstition."

Shaw was an outspoken critic and it is not surprising to find him, throughout his life, the focus of personal and public hostility. It is one thing, however, to alienate the odd actor, composer or playwright, but quite another to alienate almost a whole nation – which is what Shaw did with his views about the 1914–18 war. It is, of course, possible to view the episode from the other side, as Churchill does in one of the extracts quoted from Great Contemporaries. But it is impossible not to admire the way in which Shaw stuck to his guns while the military were sticking to theirs. Before the war began, many socialists had discussed the idea of boycotting the war effort; but when it came to the point, nationalism proved a more emotive force than International Socialism. His pamphlet *Common Sense About the War*, it is said, earned him the epithet of Most Hated Man in England. What infuriated him most of all was the atitude of the Church: "In no previous war have we struck that top note of keen irony, the closing of the Stock Exchange and not of the Church. The pagans were more logical: they closed the Temple of Peace when they drew the sword. We turn our Temples of Peace promptly into temples of war and exhibit our parsons as the most pugnacious characters in the community."

To write this kind of thing in 1914 must have required extraordinary courage. Enthusiasm for the war lasted at least until 1916 before it was destroyed at the Somme and apart from the patriotic fervour it aroused, there were apparently good arguments for it: we stuck by Belgium, as we were to stick by Poland in World War II; and there was a widespread feeling also that this was a war on behalf of Democracy against Tyranny. What enabled Shaw to face up to the hostility he aroused?

The key to his character is that he was by birth and by nature an outsider. He was an Irishman among Englishmen, just as he had been, in Dublin, a Protestant among Catholics. This helped him to an objective view of things. But more important was his own temperament. Despite the note of arrogance and self-righteousness he assumed in his writings, he adopted towards himself the same clear-headed critical attitude that he adopted towards everyone else. There is a humility in him that is a source of great strength. He was entirely free from something many people have to contend with: what T. S. Eliot called "the endless struggle to think well of themselves". There is also a coldness about him; he appeared to have few physical and emotional needs. He was a vegetarian, a teetotaller, a non-smoker; he seems to have inspired adoration in women because although he enjoyed flirting with them, he did not need them and was proof against their charm. Hesketh Pearson recalls Shaw saying: "One day I went to a party given by Lady Kennet of the Dene. Sitting alone on a sofa, clothed in draperies and appearing rather damaged, was a woman whose face looked as if it had been made of sugar and someone had licked it. This was Isadora Duncan. We were introduced. She rose held out her arms and cried "I have loved you all my life. Come!" Well, I went. We sat together on the sofa; the entire party gathered round us as if they were witnessing a play; and for an hour we performed an act of Tristan and Isolde for their benefit. After it was over, she begged me to call on her, when she declared that she would dance for me undraped. I gravely made a note of the appointment, but forgot to keep it."

His passions were indeed simple or well under control. There is no trace in Shaw of jealousy, for example, nor malice, nor bad temper nor of conflicting emotions like love-hate. As a result he appears perfectly adjusted, without complexes or guilt feelings. Though this made Shaw invulnerable, it infuriated his enemies and Shaw was well aware of that. "My mental and moral superiority are insufferable", he told Hesketh Pearson. "No chink can be observed by the naked eye in my armour. Such a preposterous personification of repulsive virtues is intolerable."

The posthumous publication (1952) of Shaw's correspondence with Mrs. Patrick Campbell reveals the only chink known to this writer. Whereas the letters to Ellen Terry are charming blarney, the 1912–13 letters to 'Mrs. Pat' mean what they say, even when Shaw tries to pass them off as blarney. For once, it seems, Shaw the supersane man is unable to cope: he is a married man, in love with a fascinating widow, caught between his feelings and his duty as a husband. When Mrs. Campbell puts an end to it by marrying again, Shaw writes an angry and jealous letter. One wonders what might have happened if she had not done so. What would Shaw have done? He had already tried forgetting her through sheer hard work and by pretending she meant nothing to him. Neither had worked: "my first defeat" he writes, but then has the insight to add "and my first success." One possibility is that he might have discovered the limitations of his own supersanity – and this in turn might conceivably have had an interesting effect on his writing. There may indeed be such an effect in *Heartbreak House*. But this is mere speculation. What is certain is that the correspondence is the most human portrait of Shaw that exists and that Mrs. Campbell is one of the most perceptive of his critics. As she says, like the conjuror's rabbit, there does emerge 'the dear tenderness of your nature – struggling about in your heart and eyes and voice, you holding it hard by the ears but I know it can get away with you in a moment".

Shaw's later view of the affair, as he portrays it in *The Apple Cart*, is probably an attempt at rationalisation of this 'dangerous' episode. If so, it says little for Shaw. The triumph of Magnus over Orinthia reveals their creator as a prig and an egotist concerned less with truth than with self-justification.

At any rate, whatever conclusions one draws from this affair, Shaw's armour seemed impenetrable to the public eye. G. K. Chesterton said of him: "Bernard Shaw is never frivolous. He never gives his opinions a holiday; he is never irresponsible even for an instant. He had no non-sensical second self . . .';' there is no "humorous confession of futility". It is possible to argue that, like Shaw, his characters never give their opinions a holiday and that, for this reason, they possess the same coldness and apparent inhumanness. What determines the direction of a Shaw play is not a character's emotions but his intellect. What motivates Vivie in *Mrs. Warren's Profession* is not her own feelings, but her image of herself as a New Woman. She says: ". . . there are two subjects I want dropped if you don't mind. One of them is love's young dream in any shape or form: the other is the romance and beauty of life. You are welcome to any illusions you may have on these subject: I have none . . . I must be treated as a woman of business permanently single, and permanently unromantic." We, the audience, are expected to believe that this highly suspicious statement represents the whole truth about Vivie.

The final scene of *Candida* shows us the extraordinary spectacle of a wife choosing between her husband and a very young man (Marchbanks) when the audience has no reason to suppose she does not love her husband. The point of the scene is an intellectual one: to show the successful husband how much he depends on his wife. *Heartbreak House*, supposedly very different from the rest of the canon, is in reality the same. Ellie Dunn's emotions at the beginning of the play are recognisable ones. As soon as she learns what life is 'really' like, she makes all sorts of cold intellectual decisions before deciding she wants to marry the aged sea-captain Shotover (alias Bernard Shaw) because his philosophy has brought her peace. *St. Joan* is the most satisfactory of the plays, for Shaw feels no need to intellectualise Joan and is happy to accept her faith without question. It is the first time that the sceptic and the mystic – the opposite roles in Shaw's character – have met head on in one of his plays. The case for the state and the Established Church is put with all Shaw's dialectical skill: opposed to it is the voice of Joan speaking with a passion and conviction which owes nothing to any single viewpoint but to the whole of her personality. In rejecting life-imprisonment and opting for execution, Joan says

". . . to shut me from the light of the sky and the sight of the fields and flowers; to chain my feet so that I can never ride again with the soldiers nor climb the hills; to make me breathe foul damp darkness, and keep me from everything that brings me back to the love of God when your wickedness and foolishness tempt me to hate him: all this is worse than the furnace in the Bible that was heated seven times. I could do without my warhorse; I could drag about in a skirt; I could let the banners and the trumpets and the Knights and soldiers pass me and leave me behind as they leave the other women, if only I could still hear the wind in the trees, the larks in the sunshine, the young lambs crying through the healthy frost, and the blessed blessed Church bells that send my angel voices floating to me on the wind. But without these things I cannot live; and by your wanting to take them away from me, or from any human creature, I know your counsel is of the devil, and that mine is of God." – and this is a new voice in Shaw that is all too seldom heard.

Although Shaw was one of the great champions of Ibsen, one only has to compare the two writers to see how different they are, and how limited the comparison makes Shaw appear. The character, for example of Hedda Gabler is quite beyond his range, because he would never have understood why a person should wish to destroy other people – he would not have understood the passions and frustrations involved. His limitation as a playwright is that he links private people to public questions and is unwilling to consider them apart from these public questions. There is in Shaw breadth but no depth. It is his peculiar gift to entertain, instruct, stimulate – but not to satisfy. With Ibsen we feel that a clearer light has been thrown on our own confusion; with Shaw we feel that the confusion has been simplified out of existence.

Shaw is at pains to explain everything: his style is a magnificently clear scientific instrument. In his plays the writing leaves no doubts that he means exactly what he says. Poetic effects, except in St. Joan, are effects merely – embellishments. A glance at Ibsen's style will show how much is conveyed by suggestion, by tone, and by symbol . . . by contrast Shaw appears to write prose to Ibsen's poetry.

Not surprisingly, perhaps, there is now a feeling in many quarters that Shaw is dated. There is sufficient of the self-conscious iconoclast in Shaw, a sufficient whiff of the late 1890s, as Churchill says, to make one sympathise with a remark made by a colleague of mine: "To me GB Shaw is a V.B. Bore . . . I find his wit extraordinarily dated and flat now, his enfant terriblisme a petulant squeak". We have grown out of the attitudes which Shaw railed against, and his public questions are not entirely our public questions. Furthermore, much of what he said then now seems to us so obvious as not to need saying. Predictably Shaw has the answer to this: "I shall enjoy perhaps a few years' immortality. But the whirligig of time will soon bring my audiences to my point of view: and then the next Shakespeare that comes along will soon turn these petty tentatives of mine into masterpieces final for their epoch . . . it is dangerous to be hailed, as a few rash admirers have hailed me, as above all things original: what the world calls originality is only an unaccustomed method of tickling it. Meyerbeer seemed prodigiously original to the Parisians when he first burst on them. Today he is only the crow who followed Beethoven's plough. I am a crow who follows many ploughs."

Shaw may go out of fashion, may already be out of fashion. One feels, however, that, in or out, he will never disappear. Such liveliness, coupled with such purposefulness, can never fail to appeal. When one reads Shavian dialogue it is difficult not to be impressed by the nimbleness of his mind and the elegance and force of his writing, so admirably suited by its brevity and clarity to the theatre. There may indeed be limitations to Shaw, but there is always life. One may sometimes feel disenchanted with him, but to be disenchanted one must first have been enchanted with the sparkle of his wit and the vitality of his characters. Whatever the literary fashion, a play by Shaw, it seems, will always be good box office.

Neither as a musical not as a theatrical critic has he been surpassed. As a lecturer he was constantly in demand – on a wide variety of topics from theatre to religion via politics. As a letter-writer his correspondence with Ellen Terry and Mrs. Campbell shows him to be among the best in that secondary but delightful genre.

Most important of all, though he posed as a clown and *enfant terrible*, he was a serious thinker, and his success was due to his intellectual and moral energy. He faced the public issues of the day squarely, and he never gave up an unpopular viewpoint. He wrote on every conceivable subject up to the year of his death (he died in 1950 at the age of 94) and in 1944 he wrote an essay on education which is still sharp enough to make schoolmasters (or at any rate this schoolmaster) wince. Until the 1920s he had his share of unpopularity and neglect, and if thereafter he became famous and lionised (especially at the Malvern Festival created in his honour) it was no more than his due: fundamentally he was a deeply serious, responsible and unselfish figure.

"Shaw preferred the role of Devil's advocate to that of hero. He blasphemed against every god of the lip-server's idolatry, especially against Demos, the King of the Gods. This is a very unpopular game to play, and doubtless Shaw's work shows some wear and tear. But he never gave up the game, never played safe, never allowed himself to be put on the defensive. In Bernard Shaw there are no evasions, no apologies, no relaxations. Shaw has said many things which as they stand are not true. Yet he is much less deceiving than many writers with Truth on their sleeve and Facts in their filing cabinet. For he knows that the distinction is not between Truth and Untruth, but between partial truth with one motive, and partial truth with another." – Eric Bentley.

SHAW — I am a typical Irishman; my family came from Yorkshire.

G. K. CHESTERTON — If Mr. Shaw had really attempted to set out all the sensible stages of his joke, the sentence would have run something like this: that I am an Irishman is a fact of psychology which I can trace in many of the things that come out of me, my fastidiousness, my frigid fierceness and my distrust of mere pleasure. Do not start any drivelling discussions about whether the word Shaw is German or Scandinavian or Iberian or Basque. You know you are human. I know I am Irish.

SHAW — A certain Mr. Alexander Mackintosh Shaw instead of taking his pedigree for granted in the usual Shaw manner, hunted it up, and published 100 copies privately in 1877. Somebody sent me a copy; and my gratification was unbounded when I read the first sentence of the first Chapter, which ran: "It is the general tradition that the Shaws are descended of McDuff, Earl of Fife." I hastily skipped to the chapter about the Irish Shaws to make sure they were my people; and there they were, baronet and all, duly traced to the third son of that Thane of Fife who laid on and slew Macbeth. It was as good as being descended from Shakespeare, whom I had been unconsciously resolved to reincarnate from my cradle.

CHESTERTON — I may be permitted to confess that Bernard Shaw was, like other men, born. He was born in Dublin on the 26th July, 1856.

FRANK HARRIS — Bernard Shaw's Shavian grandfather was a Dublin stockbroker who had married a curate's daughter. He produced more children than profits, and on New Year's Eve, 1817, went on a spree over the birth of another son. This was George Carr Shaw. This George Carr Shaw managed to drink his way to the ripe age of forty before marrying. All we know is that, after quitting a job in an iron works, he got hold of a Government sinecure. It was such a sinecure that the office had to be abolished. The look of pain in his eyes at this bad news was too much even for politicians, so they gave him a pension of sixty pounds a year. He sold it; and it was on the proceeds of the sale that he went into business and, at forty, had the temerity to get married. The realised capital value of the pension was invested in a wholesale flour warehouse.

SHAW

He knew nothing about the flour business, and his partner, a Mr. Clibborn, knew if possible

less. They did not work the industry: it worked them. It kept alive, but did not flourish. Early in its history the bankruptcy of one of its customers dealt it such a blow that my father's partner broke down in tears. My father, albeit ruined, found the magnitude of the catastrophe so irresistibly amusing that he had to retreat hastily from the office to an empty corner of the warehouse, and laugh until he was exhausted.

FRANK HARRIS A sober man would never have tried it, but then, George Carr Shaw was not always sober.

SHAW One night, when I was still about as tall as his boots, he took me out for a walk. In the course of it I conceived a monstrous, incredible suspicion. When I got home I stole to my mother and in an awestruck whisper said to her, "Mamma, I think Papa's drunk". She turned away with impatient disgust and said, "When is he ever anything else?" I have never believed in anything since: then the scoffer began. The drunkenness was so humiliating that it would have been unendurable if we had not taken refuge in laughter. If you cannot get rid of the family skeleton, you may as well make it dance.

It says a great deal for my mother's humanity that she did not hate her children. She did not hate anybody, nor love anybody.

FRANK HARRIS This perfect young lady walked the streets of Dublin seeing nobody. She even (the supreme test) passed shop windows full of women's clothes without stopping. She loved flowers and dogs, flowers even more than people. She seemed devoid of jealousy and envy, and even of passion, so sexless in fact that it is difficult even for her son to believe that she bore two other children beside himself.

Though I was not ill-treated – my parents being incapable of any sort of inhumanity – the fact that nobody cared for me gave me a frightful self-sufficiency, or rather a power of starving on imaginary feasts, that may have delayed my development a good deal, and leaves me to this hour a treacherous brute in matters of pure affection.

My Uncle Walter, who stayed with us from time to time in the intervals of his trips across the Atlantic as a surgeon on the Inman Liners, had an extraordinary command of picturesque language, partly derived by memory from the Bible and Prayer Book, and partly natural. He was always an artist in his obscenity and blasphemy. His efforts were controlled, deliberate, fastidiously chosen and worded. But they were all the more effective in destroying all my inculcated childish reverence for the verbiage of religion, for its legends, personifications and parables. I was driven to the essentials of religion by the reduction of every factitious or fictitious element in it to the most irreverent absurdity.

I remember at that time dreaming one night that I was dead and had gone to heaven. The picture of heaven which the then established Church of Ireland had conveyed to my childish imagination was a waiting room with a pew-like bench running all round, except at one corner, where there was a door. I was, somehow, aware that God was in the next room, accessible through that door. I was seated on the bench with my ankles tightly interlaced to prevent my legs dangling, behaving myself with all my might before the grown up people. A grimly-handsome lady who usually sat in a corner seat near me in Church, and whom I believed to be thoroughly conversant with the arrangements of the Almighty, was to introduce me presently into the next room – a moment which I was supposed to await with joy and enthusiasm. Really, of course, my heart sank like lead within me at the thought; for I felt that my feeble affection of piety could not impose on Omniscience, and that one glance of that all-searching eye would discover that I had been allowed to come to heaven by mistake.

I wish to clear myself of that confusion of religion with veneration which enables most men to imagine themselves religious when they are only reverent. I am myself, and always have been, as religious a man as Voltaire; but as I have also been, like him, an extremely irreverent one, most Englishmen are unable to conceive me as religious.

NARRATOR In his play *Major Barbara* Shaw's theme is the inadequacy of a religion which too piously concentrates upon the next world at the expense of the present one. Barbara, a major in the Salvation Army, has just escorted her millionaire arms-manufacturer father round the Salvation Army shed. Mrs Baines, her superior officer, broaches the subject of money. . . .

BARBARA Have we got money to keep the shelter open?

MRS. BAINES I hope we shall have enough to keep all the shelter open. Lord Saxmundham has promised us five thousand pounds if five other gentlemen will give a thousand each to make it up to ten thousand . . . Oh Mr. Undershaft, you have some very rich friends. Can't you help us towards the other five thousand?

BARBARA Are you really going to take this money?

MRS. BAINES Why not, dear?

BARBARA Mrs. Baines, do you know what my father is? Have you forgotten that Lord Saxmundham is Sir Horace Bodger, the whisky man? Do you remember how we implored the County Council to stop him from writing Bodger's Whisky in letters of fire against the sky; so that the poor drink-minded creatures on the Embankment could not wake up from their snatches of sleep without being reminded of their deadly thirst by that wicked sky sign? Do you know that the worst thing I have had to fight here is not the devil, but Bodger and his whisky?

MRS. BAINES Dear Barbara, will there be less drinking or more if all those poor souls we are saving come tomorrow and find the doors of our shelter shut in their faces? Lord Saxmundham gives us the money to stop drinking – to take his own business from him.

UNDERSHAFT (*sardonically gallant*) Mrs. Baines, you are irresistible. I can't disappoint you, and I can't deny myself the satisfaction of making Bodger pay up. You shall have your five thousand pounds. (*He takes out his cheque book.*)

(*As he makes out the cheque.*) But I also, Mrs. Baines, may claim a little disinterestedness. Think of my cannon foundry and my gunpowder business! think of the widows and orphans! the men and lads torn to pieces! (*Mrs. Baines shrinks; but he goes on remorselessly*) the oceans of blood, not one drop of which is shed in a really just cause! the ravaged crops! the peaceful peasants forced to till their fields under the fire of opposing armies on pain of starvation! the bad blood of the fierce little cowards at home who egg on others to fight for their national vanity. All this makes money for me: I am never richer, never busier than when the papers are full of it. Well, it is your work to preach peace on earth and goodwill towards men. (*Mrs. Baines' face lights up again.*) Every convert you make is a vote against war. (*Her lips move in prayer.*) Yet I give you this money to help you to hasten my own commercial ruin. (*He gives her the cheque.*)

MRS. BAINES (*her eyes full of tears*) Barbara, do you think I am wrong to take the money?

BARBARA No, no: God help you, dear, you must: you are saving the Army. (*She takes the silver S brooch from her collar.*)

MRS. BAINES Barbara: what are you doing?

Next day at Undershaft's Gunpowder Factory.

BARBARA Before I joined the Salvation Army, I was in my own power, and the consequence was that I never knew what to do with myself. When I joined it, I had not time enough for all the things I had to do.

UNDERSHAFT Just so: and why was that, do you suppose?

BARBARA Yesterday I should have said, because I was in the power of God. But you came and shewed me that I was in the power of Bodger and Undershaft. Today I feel – Oh, how can I put it into words. Sarah: do you remember the earthquake at Cannes, when we were little children? – how little the surprise of the first shock mattered compared to the dread and horror of waiting for the second? That is how I feel in this place today. I stood on the rock I thought eternal; and without a word of warning it reeled and crumbled under me. I was safe with infinite wisdom watching me, an army marching to Salvation with me; and in a moment, at a stroke of your pen in a cheque book, I stood alone; and the heavens were empty. That was the first shock of the earthquake. I am waiting for the second.

UNDERSHAFT Come, come, my daughter! don't make too much of your little tinpot tragedy. What do we do here when we spend years of work and thought and thousand of pounds of solid cash on a new gun or an aerial battleship. That turns out just a hairsbreadth wrong after all? Scrap it. Scrap it without wasting another hour or another pound on it. Well, you have made for yourself something that you call a morality or a religion or what not. It doesn't fit the facts. Well, scrap it. Scrap it, and get one that does fit. That is what is wrong with the world at present. It scraps its obsolete steam engines and dynamos; but it won't scrap its old prejudices and its old moralities and its old religious and its old political constitutions. If your old religion broke down yesterday, get a newer and better one for tomorrow.

BARBARA Oh how gladly I would take a better one to my soul! But you offer me a worse one. (*Turning on him with sudden vehemence.*) Justify yourself: show me some light through the darkness of this dreadful place, with its beautifully clean workshops, and respectable workmen, and model homes.

UNDERSHAFT Cleanliness and respectability do not need justification, Barbara: they justify themselves. I see no darkness here, no dreadfulness. In your Salvation shelter, I saw poverty, misery, cold, hunger. You gave them bread and treacle and dreams of heaven. I give from thirty shillings a week to twelve thousand a year. They find their own dreams: but I look after the drainage.

BARBARA And their souls?

UNDERSHAFT I save their souls, just as I saved yours.

BARBARA You saved my soul! What do you mean?

UNDERSHAFT I fed you and clothed you and housed you. I took care that you should have money enough to live handsomely – more than enough, so that you could be wasteful, careless, generous. I saved your soul from the seven deadly sins.

BARBARA (*bewildered*) The seven deadly sins!

UNDERSHAFT Yes, the deadly seven. (*Counting on his fingers*) Food, clothing, firing, rent, taxes, respectability and children. Nothing can lift those seven millstones from man's neck but money; and the spirit cannot soar until the millstones are lifted. I lifted them from your spirit. I enabled Barbara to become Major Barbara, and I saved her from the crime of poverty.

CUSINS Do you call poverty a crime?

UNDERSHAFT The worst of crimes. All the other crimes are virtues beside it: all the other dishonours are chivalry itself by comparison. Poverty blights whole cities; spreads horrible pestilences; strikes dead the very souls of all who come within sight, sound, or smell of it. What you call a crime is nothing: a murder here and a theft there, a blow now, and a curse then: what do they matter? They are only the accidents and illnesses of life. There are not fifty genuine professional criminals in London. But there are millions of poor people, abject people, dirty people, ill-fed, ill-clothed people. They poison us morally and physically, they kill the happiness of our society: they force us to do away with our own liberties and to organise unnatural cruelties for fear they should rise against us and drag us down to their abyss. Only fools fear crime: we all fear poverty.

SHAW

We are apt to picture God as an elderly gentleman with a beard, whereas he ought to be typified as an eternally young man. Matthew Arnold said that most Englishmen's idea of the Trinity was three Lord Shaftesburys.

CHESTERTON

Shaw is like Swift in combining extravagant fancy with a curious sort of coldness. I incline to think myself that the Catholic Church has added charity and gentleness to the virtues of a people which would otherwise have been too keen and contemptuous, too aristocratic. But however this may be there can surely be no question that Bernard Shaw's Protestant education in a Catholic country has made a great deal of difference to his mind. It has affected it in two ways, the first negative and the second positive. It has affected him by cutting him off from the fields and fountains of his real home and history – Mr. Shaw has no living traditions, no schoolboy tricks, no college customs to link him with other men. And it has affected him by the particular colour of the particular religion which he received; by making him a Puritan.

NARRATOR

At the age of 10, Shaw was sent to the Wesleyan Connexional School in Dublin.

SHAW

I did not learn anything at school. None of my schoolmasters really cared a rap (or perhaps it would be fairer to them to say that their employers did not care a rap and therefore did not give them the necessary caning powers) whether I learnt my lessons or not, provided my father paid the schooling bill, the collection of which was the real object of the school. In order to get expelled it was necessary to commit a crime of such atrocity that the parents of the other boys would have threatened to remove their sons sooner than allow them to be schoolfellows with the delinquent. I can remember only one case in which such a penalty was threatened; and in that case the culprit, a boarder, had kissed a housemaid, or possibly, being a handsome youth, had been kissed by her. She did not kiss me; and nobody ever dreamt of expelling me.

It is sometimes remarked that the school dunce often turns out well afterwards, as if idleness were a sign of ability and character. A much more sensible explanation is that the so-called dunces are not exhausted before they begin the serious business of life.

When a man teaches something he does not know to someone else who has no aptitude for it, and gives him a certificate of proficiency, the latter has completed the education of a gentleman.

NARRATOR The musical activities of his family were the most important part of his education.

SHAW My mother's salvation came through music. She had a mezzo-soprano voice of extraordinary purity of tone; and to cultivate it she took lessons from George John Vandaleur Lee, already well established in Dublin as an orchestral conductor, an organiser of concerts, and a teacher of singing so heterodox and original that he depended for his performances on amateurs trained by himself, and was detested by his professional rivals. His influence in our household, of which he at last became a member, accustomed me to the scepticism as to academic authority which still persists in me.

FRANK HARRIS — This came very shortly to be Mrs. Shaw's religion. It would be easy to hint that she swallowed his technique of singing known in the Shaw houshold as The Method to get at Lee. But the fact is that she was through with men as men. The bond between Lee and her was The Method.

SHAW — It is surely a better education for a boy to know Beethoven's Sonatas well enough to whistle them than to know the Odes of Horace well enough to recite them. In my small-boyhood I by good luck had an opportunity of learning Don Giovanni thoroughly, and if it were only for the sense of the value of the workmanship which I gained from it, I should still esteem that lesson the most important of my education. My first childish doubt as to whether God could really be a good Protestant was suggested by my observation of the deplorable fact that the best voices available for combination with my mother's in the works of the great composers had been unaccountably vouchsafed to Roman Catholics. Even the divine gentility was presently called in question, for some of these vocalists were undeniably connected with retail trade. If religion is that which binds men to one another, and irreligion that which sunders, then must I testify that I found the religion of my country in its musical genius and its irreligion in its Churches and drawing rooms.

FRANK HARRIS — Vandaleur Lee at last got his foot into England at a country house in Shropshire, where the lady fancied herself as an amateur prima donna; and he made smart acquaintances there. He had always said that he would take a house in Park Lane; and he did.

SHAW — When it was clear that he was going to stay

there and that Dublin had seen the last of him our house in Hatch Street had to be given up. So my mother took a London house in Victoria Grove, way down the Fulham Road, and settled there with her two daughters, whilst I and my father went into Dublin lodgings at 61 Harcourt Street. This must have been somewhere around 1871.

FRANK HARRIS

In 1871 Shaw entered Uniacke Townshend's land office in Dublin and stayed there five years. He began as a junior clerk. The place was overstaffed with gentlemen – apprentices who paid high premiums for receiving operatic instruction from Shaw when the boss was out. The Miserere scene from *Il Trovatore* was their favourite. Shaw very reluctantly accepted an obligation not to discuss religion with them, as his views on that subject were too subversive for so select an office. A year later the cashier, the most reponsible functionary in the office, had to leave suddenly. In this emergency the youthful Shaw was tried as a stopgap. He made good, was raised to £48 a year and bought a tail coat. Things were going splendidly for him, and his father, now at last really a teetotaller, began to see blossoming the success he himself might have been. But Shaw himself loathed his servitude, and was only waiting to escape, not only from the office, but from Dublin to London, where alone at that time an artistic career was possible.

SHAW

Behold me therefore in my twentieth year, with a business training in an occupation which I detested as cordially as any sane person lets himself detest anything he cannot escape from. In March 1876 I broke loose. I gave a month's notice. My employers naturally thought I was discontented with my salary and explained to me quietly that they hoped to make my

position more eligible. My only fear was that they should make it so eligible that all excuse for throwing it up would be taken from me. After enjoying for a few days the luxury of not having to go to the office, and being, if not my own master, at least not anyone else's slave, I packed a carpet bag; boarded the North Wall boat; and left the train next morning at Euston, where, on hearing a porter cry, in an accent quite strange to me (I had hardly ever heard an h dropped before) "Ensm' faw weel?" which I rightly interpreted as "Hansom or four wheel?" I was afraid to say hansom, because I had never been in one and was not sure that I should know how to get in. So I solemnly drove in a growler to Victoria Grove.

CHESTERTON Bernard Shaw entered England as an alien, as an invader, as a conqueror. In other words he entered England as an Irishman.

NARRATOR In Shaw's play *The Man of Destiny* Shaw depicted an alien who wished to invade and conquer, Napoleon.

NAPOLEON The English are a race apart. No Englishman is too low to have scruples: no Englishman is high enough to be free from their tyranny. But every Englishman is born with a certain miraculous power that makes him master of the world. When he wants a thing, he never tells himself that he wants it. He waits patiently until there comes into his mind, no one knows how, a burning conviction that it is his moral and religious duty to possess the thing he wants. Then he becomes irresistible. Like the aristocrat, he does what pleases him and grabs what he covets: like the shopkeeper, he pursues his purpose with the industry and steadfastness that come from strong religious conviction and deep sense of moral responsibility. He is never at a loss for an effective moral attitude. As the great champion of freedom and national independence, he conquers and annexes half the world, and calls it Colonisation. When he wants a new market for his adulterated Manchester goods, he sends a missionary to teach the natives the Gospel of Peace. The natives kill the missionary: he flies to arms in defence of Christianity; fights for it; conquers for it; and takes the market as a reward from heaven.

FRANK HARRIS

On joining his mother and sister in London he allowed himself to be pushed into one more commercial job. He was employed by the Edison Telephone Company, and after a brief but irksome experience of persuading all sorts and conditions of London shopkeepers to allow telephone wires to be attached to their premises he was made manager of his department. When the company was bought up by the Bell Telephone Company, he seized the opportunity to break loose and settled down to write novels.

SHAW

I was an able-bodied and able-minded young man in the strength of my youth; and my family, then heavily embarrassed, needed my help urgently. That I should have chosen to be a burden to them instead was, according to all the conventions of peasant lad fiction, monstrous. Well, without a blush I embraced the monstrosity. I did not throw myself into the struggle for life: I threw my mother into it.

CHESTERTON

He began by writing novels. They are not much read, and indeed not imperatively worth reading, with one exception of the crude and magnificent *Cashel Byron's Profession*.

SHAW

I never think of *Cashel Byron's Profession* without a shudder at the narrowness of my escape from becoming a successful novelist at the age of twenty-six. At that moment an adventurous publisher might have ruined me.

CHESTERTON Mr. William Archer, the distinuished theatre critic, in the course of his kindly efforts on behalf of his young Irish friend, sent this book to Samoa, for the opinion of the most elvish and yet efficient of modern critics, R. L. Stevenson, who summed up much of Shaw even from that fragment.

STEVENSON A romantic griffin roaring with laughter at the nature of his own quest.

CHESTERTON He also added the not wholly unjustified postscript:

STEVENSON I say Archer – my God, what women!

SHAW I had no success as a novelist. I sent the five novels to all the publishers in London and some in America. None would venture on them. Fifty or sixty refusals without a single acceptance forced me into a fierce self-sufficiency. I became undiscourageable, acquiring a superhuman insensitiveness to praise or blame which has been useful to me since. I was left without a ray of hope; yet I did not stop writing novels until, having planned my fifth effort, *An Unsocialist Socialist*, on a colossal scale, I found at the end of what were to me only the first two sections of it, that I had no more to say, and had better wait until I had educated myself much farther.

I was also painfully shy, and was simply afraid to accept invitations, with the result that I very soon ceased to get any.

NARRATOR Possibly because of his sister, who sang beautifully, he got to know Lady Wilde, at one of whose receptions Oscar Wilde went and spoke to him with the evident intention of being specially kind.

SHAW We put each other out frightfully; and this odd difficulty persisted between us to the very last. I saw him very seldom, as I avoided literary and artistic coteries like the plague, and refused with burlesque ferocity the few invitations I received to go into society, so as to keep out of it without offending people past their willingness to indulge me as a privileged lunatic.

NARRATOR Oscar Wilde on Shaw . . .

WILDE An excellent man; he has not an enemy in the world, and none of his friends like him.

NARRATOR Robert Ross . . .

ROSS I once met Shaw in Chartres Cathedral. He asked me to take him round and tell him everything I knew about the stained-glass windows. By dint of relentless examination he pumped me dry of every scrap of information I possessed, and at the end of an hour I was fit only for a turkish bath and alcoholic stimulants. Now Oscar would have told me wonderful stories about those windows – all made up on the spur of the moment, of course – and at the end of an hour I should still have been begging for more.

CHESTERTON Bernard Shaw is never frivolous. He never gives his opinions a holiday; he is never irresponsible even for an instant. He has no nonsensical second self which he can get into as one gets into a dressing-gown; that ridiculous disguise which is yet more real than the real person. That collapse and humorous confession of futility was much of the force in Charles Lamb and in Stevenson. There is nothing of

this in Shaw; his wit is never a weakness; therefore it is never a sense of humour.

NARRATOR Most of Shaw's acquaintances were less presentable.

CHESTERTON When he first went to London he mixed with every kind of revolutionary society, and met every kind of person except the ordinary person. He knew everybody, so to speak, except everybody. He was more than once a momentary apparition among the respectable atheists. He knew Bradlaugh and spoke on the platforms of that Hall of Science in which very simple and sincere masses of men used to hail with shouts of joy the assurance that they were not immortal.

SHAW When I came to London I found people in a very curious state as regards their religious beliefs. This was illustrated by something that happened at a bachelor party I attended in Kensington a short time after I arrived. I found myself in the company of a number of young men, and they got into a dispute about religion. At that time the late Charles Bradlaugh was very notorious for a campaign he was carrying on as an atheist. One of the persons present, representing what was supposed to be the pious and religious side in the controversy, accused Bradlaugh of having publicly taken out his watch and challenged the Almighty, if he had the power and will to do so, to strike him dead within five minutes. An admirer and adherent of Bradlaugh vehemently denied the story, saying it was a gross calumny. I said that if the question which Charles Bradlaugh was dealing with was whether a God of that kind existed, the reported experiment seemed to me perfectly legitimate. I said "Since it appears that Mr. Bradlaugh never made this experiment, I, regarding it as a perfectly legitimate one, will try it myself", and with that I took my watch out of my pocket.

I have never done anything in public or private which produced such an instantaneous and extraordinary effect. Up to that moment the company had been divided into a pious and a sceptical party, but it now appeared that there were no sceptics present at all. Everyone of them felt it to be extremely probable that before the five minutes were up I should be taken at my word. One of the party appealed to us to turn the conversation to a more lively channel, and a gentleman present who had a talent for singing comic songs sat down at the piano and sang the most melancholic comic song I ever heard in my life.

NARRATOR From 1876 to 1885 the Shaws lived in poverty.

SHAW I remember once buying a book entitled *How to Live on Sixpence a Day,* a point on which at that time circumstances compelled me to be pressingly curious. My main reason for adopting literature as a profession was, that as the author is never seen by his clients, he need not dress respectably.

NARRATOR Shaw's struggles, however, were over by 1885.

SHAW I never struggled. I rose by sheer gravitation.

NARRATOR In 1879 he had joined a Debating Club called the Zetetical Society, whose members discussed Religious and Philosophical topics. Terrified by the prospect of speaking in public, Shaw was determined to overcome his nerves by speaking as often as possible.

SHAW I was like an officer afflicted with cowardice, who takes every opportunity of going under fire to get over it and learn his business.

NARRATOR

In 1884 Shaw joined the Fabian Society. Its original intention had been to reform society "in accordance with the highest moral possibilities" and to found a colony in Brazil. The more intelligent and influential of its members broke away from the original circle to found a society of socialists bent on a reform of English political life by the gradual process of discussion and persuasion. Shaw joined in May 1884, and was elected to the executive in January 1885.

SHAW

Other Socialist bodies usually proposed to enlist everybody except the capitalists in their own ranks. Their programme was: "We will explain our good intentions and our sound economic basis to the whole world; the whole world will then join us at a subscription of a penny a week; then the whole of society belonging to our society, we shall become society, and we shall proceed to take the government of the country into our hands, and we shall inaugurate the millennium". But what disabled them was that the world wouldn't come in.

The Fabian Society set its face against that from the beginning. The Fabian Society said that its sound should go out into all lands, but it did not say that everybody else's sound should come into its own little penny trumpet. The Fabian was a man who was never urged to join the Fabian Society. In fact, when he first tried to do it he usually found some difficulty.

NARRATOR

One of those who found no difficulty in entering the Fabian Society, and was actually persuaded to join by Shaw, was Sidney Webb. He was an Upper Division Civil Servant whom Shaw had first met at the meetings of the Zetetical Society. He was to become a pillar of the Fabian establishment and a chief architect of the Labour Party's Reform Programme of 1918, with his wife Beatrice, whose personal

fortune enabled them to live independently. It was an ideal marriage. They were described as "two typewriters clicking as one."

SHAW Each of us was the other's complement. He knew everything that I didn't know; and I knew everything that he didn't know, which was precious little. He was competent: I was incompetent. He was politically and administratively experienced: I was a novice. He was extraordinarily able and quite respectable: I was a futile Bohemian. He was an indefatigable investigator: I was an intuitive guesser. I was an artist and a metaphysician: to him I was in both capacities a freak, but a clever, amusing and curable one. Above all he was simple, single and solid, always true to himself. He was at all points the very collaborator I needed; and I just grabbed him.

NARRATOR The Webbs' scientific attitude to socialism was too much for a later member of the Fabian Society, H. G. Wells, who said of Mrs. Webb.

WELLS She saw men as samples moving.

NARRATOR And of the Fabians of the future as envsiaged by Sidney Webb.

WELLS Admirable Webblets, mysteriously honest, brightly efficient, bustling virtuously about their carefully involved duties and occasionally raising a neatly rolled umbrella to check the careless course of some irregular citizen who had forgotten to button up his imagination or shave his character.

NARRATOR The Fabians disagreed with the Marxists and were, like the Labour Party, condemned by them. With reservations, Shaw agreed with Marx that a situation where the rich lived off the unearned income produced by rent and dividends was intolerable. His first recorded public speech, made in January 1885 at the Industrial Remuneration Conference, begins:

SHAW

It is the desire of the President that nothing shall be said that might give pain to particular classes. I am about to refer to a modern class, burglars, and if there is a burglar present I beg him to believe that I cast no reflection upon his profession. I am not unmindful of his great skill and enterprise; his risks, so much greater than those of the most speculative capitalist, extending as they do to risk of liberty and life; nor do I overlook his value to the community as an employer on a large scale, in view of the criminal lawyers, policeman, turnkeys, gaol builders and sometimes hangmen that owe their livelihoods to his daring undertakings. I hope any shareholders and landlords who may be present will accept my assurance that I have no more desire to hurt their feelings than to give pain to burglars: I merely wish to point out that all three inflict on the community an injury of precisely the same nature.

NARRATOR

Shaw disliked Landlords and Shareholders because he disliked unearned income, which allowed manpower to go to waste.

CHESTERTON

When taxed in a *Daily News* discussion with being a socialist for the obvious reason that poverty was cruel, he said this was quite wrong; it was only because poverty was wasteful. The truth is that Shaw only took this economic pose from his hatred of appearing sentimental. If Bernard Shaw killed a dragon rescued a princess of romance, he would try to say "I have saved a princess" with exactly the same intonation as "I have saved a shilling".

CHESTERTON

His great defect, however, is the lack of democratic sentiment. There is nothing demo-

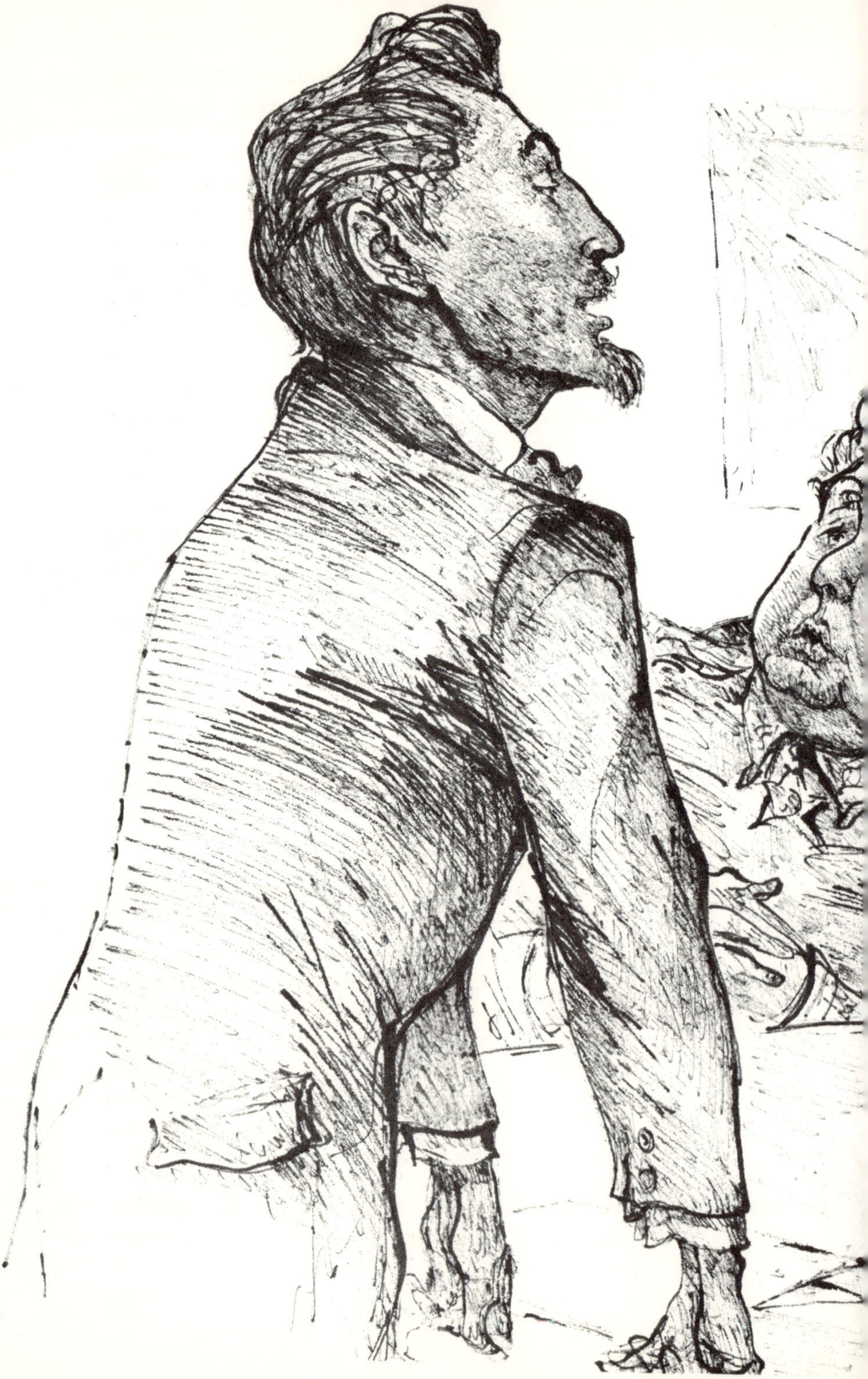

cratic either in his humanitarianism or his Socialism.

SHAW Government by the people is not and never can be a reality: it is only a cry by which demagogues humbug us into voting for them. If you doubt this – if you ask me "Why should not the people make their own laws?" I need only ask you "Why should not the people write their own plays?" They cannot. It is much easier to write a good play than to make a good law. And there are not a hundred men in the world who can write a play good enough to stand daily wear and tear as long as a law must. When we have what is called a popular movement very few people who take part in it know what it is all about. I once saw a real popular movement in London. People were running excitedly through the streets. Everyone who saw them doing it immediately joined in the rush. They ran simply because everyone else was doing it. It was most impressive to see thousands of people sweeping along at full speed like that. There could be no doubt that it was literally a popular movement. I ascertained afterwards that it was started by a runaway cow. That cow had an important share in my education as a political philosopher.

NARRATOR And in one of his late plays, *The Apple Cart*, when there is a power-struggle between the king and his democratically-elected cabinet, Shaw is clear which side he is on.

PROTEUS (*Impressively eloquent*) At this moment my cue is to show you, not my own temper, but the temper of my cabinet. What the Foreign Secretary and the Chancellor of the Exchequer and the Home Secretary have told you is true. If we are to carry on your government we cannot have you making speeches that express your own opinions and not ours. We cannot have you implying that everything that is of any value in our legislation is your doing and not ours. We cannot have you telling people that their only safeguard against the political encroachments of big business whilst we are doing nothing but bungling and squabbling is your power of veto. It has got to stop, once for all.

BALBUS }
NICOBAR } Hear Hear!

PROTEUS Is that clear?

MAGNUS Far clearer than I have ever dared to make it, Mr. Proteus. Except by the way, on one point. When you say that all this of which you complain must cease once for all, do you mean that henceforth I am to agree with you or you with me?

PROTEUS I mean that when you disagree with us you are to keep your disagreement to yourself.

MAGNUS That would be a very heavy responsibility for me. If I see you leading the nation over the edge of a precipice may I not warn it?

BALBUS It is our business to warn it, not yours.

MAGNUS Suppose you don't do your business! Suppose you don't see the danger! That has happened. It may happen again.

CRASSUS (*Insinuatingly*) As democrats, I think we are bound to proceed on the assumption that such a thing cannot happen.

BOANERGES Rot! It's happening all the time until somebody has the gumption to put his foot down and stop it.

CRASSUS Yes: I know. But that is not democracy.

BOANERGES Democracy be – (*he leaves the word unspoken*)! I have thirty years' experience of democracy. So have most of you. I say no more.

BALBUS Wages are too high, if you ask me. Anybody can earn from five to twenty pounds a week now, and a big dole when there is no job for him. And what Englishman will give his mind to politics as long as he can afford to keep a motor car?

NICOBAR How many voted at the last election? Not seven per cent of the register.

BALBUS Yes; and the seven per cent were only a parcel of sillies playing at ins and outs. To make democracy work in Crassus' way we need poverty and hardship.

PROTEUS (*Emphatically*) And we have abolished poverty and hardship. That is why the people trust us. (*To the king*) And that is why you will have to give way to us. We have the people of England in comfort – solid and middle class comfort – at our backs.

MAGNUS No: we have not abolished poverty and hardship. Our big businessmen have abolished them. But how? By sending our capital abroad to places where poverty and hardship still exist: in other words, where labour is cheap. We live in comfort on the imported profits of that capital. We are all ladies and gentlemen now.

NICOBAR Well, what more do you want? (*Rising*) Own the truth. You had rather have the people poor, and pose as their champion and saviour, than have to admit that the people are better off under our government – under our squabbling and bungling, as you call it.

MAGNUS No: it was the Prime Minister who used those expressions.

If I do not stand above the people there is no longer any reasons for my existence at all. I stand for the great abstractions: for conscience and virtue; for the eternal against the expedient; for the evolutionary appetite against the day's gluttony; for intellectual integrity, for humanity, for the rescue of industry from commercialism and of science from professionalism, for everything that you desire as sincerely as I, but which in you is held in leash by the Press, which can organise against you the ignorance and superstition, the timidity and credulity, the gullibility and prudery, the hating and hunting instinct of the voting mob, and cast you down from power if you utter a word to alarm or displease the adventurers who have the Press in their pockets. Between you and that tyranny stands the throne. I have no elections to fear; and if any newspaper magnate dares offend me, that magnate's fashionable wife and marriageable daughters will soon make him understand that the king's displeasure is still a sentence of social death within range of St. James's Palace. Think of the things you dare not do! the persons you dare not offend! Well, a king with a little courage may tackle them for you. I ask you, before you play your last card and destroy me, to consider where you will be without me.

NARRATOR To Shaw Democracy is something that can only exist in any real sense when the human race has improved itself.

SHAW The one danger before us that nothing can avert but a general raising of human character is the danger created by inventing weapons capable of destroying civilisation faster than we produce men who can be trusted to use them wisely.

NARRATOR Shaw's political position in the 1930s was thought by some to be pro-Mussolini and pro-Hitler. That his statements in favour of the Dictators were made to annoy, as much as anything else, is clear from this:

SHAW Nowdays the Capitalist cry is "Nationalise what you like; municipalise all you can; turn the courts of justice into courts martial and your parliaments and corporations into boards of directors with your most popular mob orators in the chair, provided the rent, the interest, and the profits come to us as before, and the proletariat still gets nothing but its keep."

This is the great corruption of Socialism which threatens us at present. It calls itself Fascism in Italy, National Socialism (Nazi for short) in Germany, New Deal in the United States, and is clever enough to remain nameless in England; but everywhere it means the same thing: Socialist production and Unsocialist distribution. So far, out of the frying pan into the fire.

NARRATOR Then, finally, what of the Labour Party, for which the Fabian Society prepared the ground?

SHAW The Labour Party is good in that it represents Labour, but bad in that it represents poverty and ignorance, and it is anti-social in that it supports the producer against the consumer and the worker against the employer instead of supporting the worker against the idlers. The Labour Party is also bad on account of its false democracy, which substitutes the mistrust, fear and political incapacity of the masses for genuine political talent, and which would make the people legislators instead of leaving them what they are at present, the judges of the legislators.

NARRATOR Shaw remained on the executive body of the Fabian Society for over thirty years – until its original aims had been fulfilled. He resisted any call to become an M.P.

SHAW Better a leader of Fabianism than a chorus man in Parliament.

NARRATOR Instead he spoke at hundreds of political meetings and clubs, asking no fee except the price of his railway ticket. He became an excellent debater and was particularly good with his questions. On one occasion he had just finished a lecture on "Flogging as a Punishment" when a parson got up to say:

PARSON In the army many men guilty of misdemeanours ask to be flogged. What has the lecturer to say to that?

SHAW The subject of my lecture was "Flogging as a Punishment" not "Flogging as a Luxury".

NARRATOR His fees for writing were not so slight. He insisted on being paid what he thought his pieces were worth, as much as anything to protect other lesser-known writers. Here is an exchange of letters between Shaw and the Editor of the *Daily Chronicle*.

EDITOR Dear Sir, I am directed by the Editor to inform you that he will see you damned before he gives you more than five pounds for the article in question.

SHAW Dear Sir, please inform the Editor that I will see him and you and the whole *Chronicle* staff boiled in Hell before I will do it for that money.

NARRATOR From May 1888 to May 1890 Shaw got a job with the London evening paper, *The Star*, to write music criticism under the pseudonym of Corno di Basseto. He subsequently did the same thing for *The World* until 1894.

SHAW

Never in my life have I penned an impartial criticism; and I hope I never may. Criticism cannot give an absolutely true and just account of any artist; it can at best explain its point of view and then describe the artist from that point of view. A criticism written without personal feeling is not worth reading. When my critical mood is at its height, personal feeling is not the word: it is passion: the passion for artistic perfection. The true critic is the man who becomes your personal enemy on the sole provocation of a bad performance . . .

NARRATOR

Composers like Hubert Parry do not think much of Shaw's music criticism. The following extract may explain why:

SHAW

For some time past I have been carefully dodging Dr. Hubert Parry's *Job*. I had presentiments about it from the first. I foresaw that all the other critics would cleverly imply that they thought it the greatest oratorio of ancient or modern times – that Handel is rebuked, Mendelssohn eclipsed, and the rest nowhere. And I was right: they did. The future historian of music, studying the English papers of 1892–3, will learn that these years produced two entire and perfect chrysolites, Parry's *Job* and Verdi's *Falstaff*, especially *Job*. I was so afraid of being unable to concur unreservedly in the verdict that I lay low and stopped my ears. The first step was to avoid the Gloucester Festival. That gave me no trouble: nothing is easier than not to go to Gloucester.

Unluckily I went last Wednesday to the concert of the Middlesex Choral Union, where

the first thing that happened was the appearance of Dr. Parry amid the burst of affectionate applause which always greets him. That made me uneasy; and I was not reassured when he mounted the conductor's rostrum, and led the band into a prelude which struck me as being a serious set of footnotes to the bridal march from *Lohengrin*. Presently up got Mr.

Bantock Pierpoint and sang, without a word of warning, There was a man in the land of Uz whose name was Job. Then I knew I was in for it; and now I must do my duty.

I take *Job* to be, on the whole, the most utter failure ever achieved by a thoroughly respectworthy musician. There is not one bar that comes within fifty thousand miles of the poem. This is the naked unexaggerated truth. Is anybody surprised at it? Here, on the one hand, is an ancient poem which has lived from civilisation to civilisation, and has been translated into an English version of haunting beauty and nobility of style, offering to the musician a subject which would have taxed to the utmost the powers of Bach, Handel, Mozart, Beethoven, or Wagner. Here on the other is, not Bach nor Handel nor Mozart nor Beethoven nor Wagner, not even Mendelssohn or Schumann, but Dr. Hubert Parry, an enthusiastic and popular professor, forty-five years old, and therefore of ascertained powers.

The most conspicuous failure in the work is Satan, who, after a feeble attempt to give himself an infernal air by getting the bassoon to announce him with a few frog-like croaks, gives up the pretence, and, though a tenor and a fiend, models himself on Mendelssohn's St. Paul.

As to Job, there is no sort of grit in him: he is abject from first to last, and is only genuinely touching when he longs to lie still and be quiet where the wicked cease from troubling and the weary are at rest. He is much distracted by fragments of themes from the best composers coming into his head from time to time, and sometimes cutting off the thread of his discourse altogether.

Not until he has given in completely, and is saying his last word, does it suddenly occur to him to make a hit; and then, in announcing that he repents in dust and ashes, he explodes in the most unlooked-for way on the final word 'ashes', which produces the effect of a sneeze. The expostulation of God with Job is given to the chorus: the voice that sometimes speaks through the mouths of babes and sucklings here speaks through the mouths of Brixton and Bayswater, and the effect is precisely what might have been expected. It is the old academic story – an attempt to bedizen a dramatic poem with scraps of sonata music.

FRANK HARRIS No doubt Shaw's music criticism made funny reading. A few thousand unmusical stockbrokers and deaf mutes had a good laugh at it. But no critic of the *theatre* has matched Shaw since his time, except possibly George Jean Nathan. They both wrote with an air of men who were crammed with facts and who threw them overboard in sackloads in order to increase their speed.

NARRATOR In January 1895 Shaw began to criticise the drama in *The Saturday Review* at a salary of £6 a week. His new editor was Frank Harris.

SHAW I told myself that this was the man for me as an editor, but that he would bully me if I did not bully him first. My bullying was very mild. He was telling me how he had upset himself by some athletic feat on the river. I immediately assumed the character of the President of the Royal College of Physicians and said severely "Do you drink?" He was taken aback for a moment. Then he accepted the situation and gave me quite a long account of his symptoms.

NARRATOR Shaw's theatrical criticism is coloured by his view that it should be propagandist. This explains his championing of Ibsen to such an extent that he was even prepared to back him against Shakespeare.

SHAW — *A Doll's House* will be as flat as ditchwater when *A Midsummer Night's Dream* will still be fresh as paint; but it will have done more work in the world; and that is enough for the highest genius.

NARRATOR — Shaw criticised Shakespeare for having no message, for not being philosophical and for not being a master of psychological realism. He considered that Shakespeare's genius was primarily a musical one. Critics and actors were outraged but . . .

SHAW — The bardolatry I shook up was simple ignorance: the bardolaters never read him.

NARRATOR — Shaw knew Shakespeare almost by heart, far too well for the comfort for the most celebrated actor of the day, Henry Irving. His productions at the Lyceum, with Ellen Terry as his leading lady, were exploded by Shaw.

SHAW — In a true republic of art Sir Henry Irving would ere this have expiated his acting versions on the scaffold. He does not merely cut plays: he disembowels them. In *Cymbeline* he has quite surpassed himself by extirpating the antiphonal third verse of the famous dirge. A man who would do that would do anything – cut the coda out of the first movement of Beethoven's Ninth Symphony, or shorten one of Velasquez's Philips into a kitcat to make it fit over his drawing room mantelpiece.

NARRATOR — More depended on Shaw and Irving being friends than Irving's peace of mind – for caught between them was Ellen Terry.

ELLEN TERRY H and I are out! A little bit. For he don't tell me things about you, because he's vexed always with people who won't agree always and entirely with everything he says, and although I try not to aggravate him by actually *saying* so, I don't agree with him about you, and he knows it.

Don't quarrel with H. I kiss you on the tip of your innocent nose and *remain* etc., etc.

Please take me upstairs and read me by yourself.

NARRATOR But Shaw retained his most critical comments for contemporary playwrights who gave the public what it wanted, not what was good for it. This is what he had to say about the notorious Mrs. Ebbsmith, by Arthur Wing Pinero.

SHAW She is the daughter of a secularist agitator. After eight years of married life, during which she was for one year her husband's sultana, and for the other seven his housekeeper, she has emerged into widowhood and an active career as an agitator, speaking from the platforms formerly occupied by her father. Although educated, well-conducted, beautiful, and a sufficiently powerful speaker to produce a great effect in Trafalgar Square, she loses her voice from starvation, and has to fall back on nursing.

In the course of her nursing she finds a patient who falls in love with her. He is married to a shrew; and he proposes to spend the rest of his life with his nurse, preaching the horrors of marriage. She then finds out that he does not care a rap about her ideas, and that his attachment to her is simply sexual. Here we start with a dramatic theme capable of interesting development. Mr. Pinero, unable to develop it, lets it slip through his fingers after one feeble clutch at it, and proceeds to degrade his drama below the ordinary level by making the woman declare that her discovery of the nature of the man's feelings puts within her reach "the only one hour in a woman's life", in pursuance of which detestable view she puts on an indecent dress and utterly abandons herself to him. A clergyman appears at the crisis, and offers her a Bible. She promptly pitches it into the stove; and a thrill of horror runs through the audience as they see, in imagination, the whole Christian Church tottering before their eyes. Suddenly with a wild scream, she plunges her hand into the glowing stove and pulls out the Bible again. The Church is saved; and the curtain descends amid thunders of applause. In that applause I hope I need not say I did not join.

NARRATOR — By 1895, Shaw had begun his highly successful career as a playwright and was now a celebrity.

FRANK HARRIS — Shaw's first use of his affluence was the renewal of his deplorable wardrobe. The Jaeger Company (Jaeger being a German doctor with a craze for regenerating the world by all-wool clothing) opened a West-End tailoring establishment, for which the doctor designed new combined coats and waistcoats. In these Shaw hastened to vest himself, to the amazement of his friends, as the emergence of the Jaegerised butterfly from the desperately seedy chrysalis took place quite suddenly. Jaeger allowed his craze to run away with him. He designed an ideally healthy single garment in brown knitted wool, complete from sleeves to ankles in one piece, in which a human being resembled nothing but a forked radish in a worsted bifurcated stocking. As it seemed clear that no man could appear in it in a London Street without being mobbed, Shaw promptly ordered a specimen to his measure and made a trial trip in it from Tottenham Court Road to Marble Arch and back without molestation. Shaw was content with the Oxford Street test and made only one or two more public appearances in it; but at the first performance of his first play *Widowers' Houses*, Shaw stepped out before the curtain in a suit of dazzling grey stockinet and told the booing multitude what he thought of it.

The smart-looking stockinet soon had to be discarded because it stridulated so frightfully, as the wearer's arms swung against his sides as he walked, that Lord Olivier, hiking in the country with Shaw, objected to his companion drowning his conversation by making a noise like a cricket.

CHESTERTON One has come to think of the reddish-brown Jaeger suit as if it were a sort of reddish brown fur, and was, like the hair and eyebrows, a part of the animal. His brown woollen clothes, at once artistic and hygienic, completed the appeal for which he stood; which might be defined as an eccentric healthy-mindedness.

NARRATOR After a slow start, Shaw, in his thirties, realised that he was attractive to women. At first he was flattered, then irritated. He preferred flirtatious correspondence to definite love-affairs.

SHAW Love is only diversion and recreation to me. My pockets are always full of the small change of love-making; but it is magic money, not real money. I am fond of women, but I am in earnest about quite other things.

NARRATOR Shaw conducted two passionate correspondences. The first was with Ellen Terry – they met for the first time only years later. But one night at the theatre Ellen Terry peeped through the curtain when Shaw was in the audience.

ELLEN TERRY — I've seen you at last! You *are* a boy! And a Duck! And so that was you! How deadly delicate you look!

NARRATOR — The second correspondence, which was much more like a real love affair, was with the celebrated actress Mrs. Patrick Campbell, the original Eliza Doolittle. They called each other Joey and Stella.

ELLEN TERRY — And so now you love Mrs. P.C.? Well she's a very lovely lady, and clever and amusing. I've always liked her, tho' I scarcely know her.

NARRATOR — It lasted longer than 35 hours. . . . Another playwright, J. M. Barrie, who lived opposite Shaw, wrote the following in answer to a letter from Mrs. Campbell.

BARRIE — I thought when I saw your nice little monogram that it meant that you no longer adored GBS and that you had crossed the street again to me. You see, I had watched you (a bitter smile on my face) popping in at his door instead of at mine. For the moment I am elated though well I know that you will soon be off with me again and on with him. He and I live in the weather house with two doors, and you are the figure that smiles on us or turns up its nose at us alternately.

NARRATOR — In September 1912 Mrs Campbell became ill and was ordered to rest for six months. Shaw came to see her as often as he could.

SHAW — This thing is getting ridiculous. Yesterday I was almost free: now your letter brings everything back to me again and makes a baby of me. . . . Here I am caught up again, breathless, with no foothold, at a dizzy height, in an ecstasy which must be delirious and presently end in my falling headlong to destruction. And yet I am happy, as madmen are. What does this sound like from me, the Supersane Man?

MRS. PATRICK CAMPBELL — I wish I was dining with you at the Ritz tonight both of us 21! – and you in evening dress and I looking lovely too! Oh no, I mean I wish it was a wet night in the park and you were speaking and I was giving away pamphlets and leading the applause. . . . Its a dreadful thought but I believe I shall suddenly jump out of bed and take a taxi to——

NARRATOR — Things were very much complicated by the fact that by 1912 Shaw was married.

SHAW — I am all torn to bits . . . our conversation was overheard; and the effect was dreadful: It hurts me miserably to see anyone suffer like that. I must, it seems, murder myself or else murder her. It will pass over; but in the meantime here is a lovely spring day murdered.

MRS. P.C. — D.D. asked me whether you made 'love' to me. I said you made 'advances'.

SHAW — Oh I must work . . . If I stop to think about myself and you the situation becomes desperate. With you I forget everything. Away from you I remember everything when I have time; so I must leave myself no time and be a machine – all I am good for.

MRS. P.C. — He walks into your heart with his muddy galoshes and then walks out leaving his muddy galoshes behind him.

SHAW I MUSTN'T be in love; but I *am*. Writing is no use. I have written everything, said everything. And I am saying it still. Only I want to say it so that you can really feel it.

I am still quite mad and quite sane and quite fifty different things all at once; but I don't want to write it now; I want to live it. I can't do anything with this pen and paper. I shall go to bed and think about it.

. . . Won't you say something to me?

No: its ridiculous to be importunate: its infernal to be expected to write. You shan't be bothered.

Still, just –

Oh, Stella!

I should like to see you most frightfully

If only –

Stella, Stella, Stella

Da Capo

And Stella, Stella, Stella Stella, Stella, Stella

And so on for a thousand bars . . .

MRS. P.C. When I was four one Christmas day a conjuror came–and out of his shiny tall hat he brought a little soft bunny–oh the joy of sweet surprise and I feel like that at all the dear Tenderness of your nature – struggling about in your heart and eyes and voice–and you holding it hard by the ears but I know it can get away with you in a moment.

NARRATOR In 1913 Mrs. Campbell contemplated a second marriage.

SHAW I want to implore you not to rouse the family solicitor in me by talking of marrying George . . . it would turn me into rusty iron and cut me off for ever from what is common and young in my humanity. Therefore, though I like George (we have the same taste) I say he is young and I am old; so let him wait until I am tired of you . . . It is impossible I should not tire soon: nothing so wonderful could last. You cannot really be what you are to me: you are a figure from the dreams of my boyhood. I promise to tire as soon as I can so as to leave you free. I will produce Pygmalion and criticise your acting. I will yawn over your adorable silly sayings and ask myself are they really amusing. I will run after other women in search of a new attachment; I will hurry through my dream as fast as I can; only let me have my dream out.

NARRATOR Nothing so wonderful *could* last. When they were both intending to stay simultaneously in Sandwich in August 1913, Mrs. Campbell wrote:

MRS. P.C. Oh you know I must be alone by the sea – how are strength and steadiness to come to me otherwise.

It's getting difficult not to love you more than I ought to love you – Offend me again quickly to pull me together – But by the sea I must be alone – you know.

NARRATOR But Shaw went all the same.

MRS. P.C. Please will you go back to London today – or go wherever you like but don't stay here – If you won't go I must – I am very very tired and I oughtn't to go another journey. Please don't make me despise you.

SHAW Very well, go: the loss of a woman is not the end of the world. The sun shines: it is pleasant to swim: it is good to work: my soul can stand alone. But I am deeply, deeply, deeply wounded. You have tried me; and you are not comfortable with me: I cannot bring you peace, or rest, or even fun: there is nothing really frank in our comradeship after all. It is I who have been happy, carelessly happy, comfortable, able to walk for miles after dinner at top speed in search of you, singing all the way. . . . You run after life furtively and run away or huddle up and scream when it turns and opens its arms to you: you are a man's disgrace and infatuation not his crown above rubies . . . you are a one-part actress and that one not a real part: you are an owl sickened by two days of my sunshine. . . .

MRS. P.C. You vagabond you – you blind man. You weaver of words, you – poor thing unable to understand a mere woman. My friend all the same. No daughters to relieve your cravings – no babes to stop your satirical chatterings.

Your letters – considering – are very well.

Do you think it was nothing to me to hurt my friend –

NARRATOR And so the affair reached its climax, although the letters continued. After World War I Shaw's reputation increased while Mrs. Campbell's declined – and her income also declined. She wished either to sell the letters for publication, or to be allowed to include them in her autobiography.

MRS. P.C. Here are the dear letters:

Both D.D. and Barrie said the letters were wonderful – and that it was generous of you to let me publish them.

People talk carelessly, but nobody would think anything but what lovely letters and what a dear man you are.

SHAW Take that terrible wadge of letters, and put it into the hands of any court of honour you can induce your fittest friends to form and they will tell you that their public exposure is utterly impossible.

MRS. P.C. If in spite of all you have said and written and allowed to be published of your private life and feelings, you still persist in refusing me your permission, do give a reason that I and the world may regard as fair and sincere.

Joey can it be that you are just modest about your own true heart – yes, I believe it is that – afraid of the best that is in you. Well, well for 76 years you have said you are God, and here you are afraid of yourself.

It's a dreadful thing to have a vaulting mind that o'erleaps itself and goes 'potty' – that's what has happened to you.

NARRATOR Shaw in return offered some suggestions as to how her autobiography might be handled: he was qualified to give her advice: he had reviewed her performances as a dramatic critic, and had produced her (she was a notorious headache for any producer) in *Pygmalion*.

SHAW What the Public want to know is not what plays and what theatres I appeared in . . . They want to know what I have to say about it all; how I justified myself for being so mad a thing as an actress at all; whether I was able to keep any real life and personality through so much mumming . . . whether I would do it again if I could begin again; why everybody adored me and nobody could stand me . . ." And a great deal more which is no business of theirs but which they nevertheless want to know.

For instance you can have a chapter on authors beginning with Henry Arthur Jones who said that you had an extraordinary sense of everything that was within 10 inches of your nose – and ending with the author who tried to seduce you when you were a brutally unprotected widow, and treated you on the stage with a brutality and savagery which you can never forget. You might even write a chapter on stage lovers from Tree, whose evening suit you stroked with passionate embraces of your heavily made-up arms until the poor man was like a zebra, to Gerald du Maurier whose outpourings of adoration on the stage you punctuated by such asides as "Good God, to have to play a scene like this to a face like that!"

NARRATOR — The letters continued until Mrs. Campbell's last year (she died in 1940). Here is a final example from 1928.

MRS. P.C. — They have asked me to play Mrs. Alving for the Ibsen Centenary, and I have accepted. You have bashed and beheaded me so often, to do it once more if you think I should ruin the play – I could get out of it.

I feel rather like the little black girl who after the Englishman kissed her, ran to her mother and said "Englishman eatee me uppee" and the next day crept back to the Englishman and said "Eatee me uppee some more".

NARRATOR — Shaw portrayed his version of their relationship in *The Apple Cart*, with himself as King Magnus, she as Orinthia.

ORINTHIA — Everyone knows that I am the real queen. Everyone treats me as the real queen. Magnus, when are you going to face my destiny and your own?

MAGNUS — But my wife? the Queen? What is to become of my poor dear Jemima?

ORINTHIA — Oh drown her: Shoot her: tell your chauffeur to drive her into the Serpentine and leave her there. The woman makes you ridiculous.

MAGNUS — Being your husband is only a job for which one man will do as well as another, and which the last man holds subject to six months notice in the divorce court. Being my wife is something quite different. The smallest derogation to Jemima's dignity would hit me like the lash of a whip across the face. It is because she is a part of my real workaday self. You belong to fairyland.

ORINTHIA Suppose she dies! Will you die too?

MAGNUS Not immediately. I shall have to carry on as best I can without her, though the prospect terrifies me.

ORINTHIA Might not carrying on without her include marrying me?

MAGNUS My dear Orinthia, I had rather marry the devil. Being a wife is not your job.

ORINTHIA You think so because you have no imagination. And you don't know me because I have never let you really possess me. I should make you more happy than any man has ever yet been on earth.

MAGNUS I defy you to make me more happy than our strangely innocent relations have already made me.

NARRATOR Shaw indeed had a wife. He married Charlotte Payne-Townshend, a rich, strong-minded Irishwoman, in 1898, despite his general attitude towards marriage. He had met her at a Fabian houseparty in Suffolk in 1896. She became his secretary in 1897.

FRANK HARRIS Shaw was, to put it mildly, not a marrying man. He was fond of quoting a saying of Nietzche's to the effect that a married philosopher is ridiculous. On the other side Miss Townshend was a strong feminist, in revolt against domestic ideals, jealous of her independence, very loth to change her name, quite prepared to defy convention, and attracted by Shaw's apparent readiness to do the same.

SHAW

Dear Ellen, I hereby testify that I, G.B.S., having this day inspected a photograph of Miss Ellen Terry, have felt all my nerves spring and my heart glow with the strongest impulse to have that lady in my arms, proving that my regard for her is a complete one, spiritual, intellectual, and physical, on all planes, at all times, under all circumstances, and for ever.

Well, shall I marry my Irish millionairess? She doesn't really *love* me. She got fond of me and did not coquet or pretend that she wasn't. I got fond of her, because she was a comfort to me. You kept my heart so warm that I got fond of everybody; and she was nearest and best. That's the situation. What does your loving wisdom say to it?

ELLEN TERRY

Somehow I think she'll love you quick enough. I *think* so, but it's what's in herself I can tell her, not what is in you. How very silly you clever people are. Fancy not knowing! Fancy not being sure! Do you know you love her?

One thing I am clever enough to know (to KNOW, mind. I know few things, but I know what I know.) It is this. You'd be all bad and no good in you, if you marry anyone unless you know you love her.

NARRATOR

Events were precipitated by an illness of Shaw's due to overwork, exhaustion and an abcess on his foot. Charlotte Payne-Townshend returned to look after him. She was quite prepared to have him move in with her, but this was not good enough for Shaw. He thought it unfair to her. So he sent her out for a ring and a licence and they were married at the West Strand Registry Office.

FRANK HARRIS — I, in my innocence, believed that people married either for love or for money. Shaw would not allow that he had married for either.

SHAW — We married because we had become indispensable to one another.

FRANK HARRIS — And that appears to be the plain truth.

NARRATOR — Winston Churchill, in his book *Great Contemporaries*, sums up Shaw at this stage:

CHURCHILL — Mr. Bernard Shaw was one of my earliest antipathies. Indeed, almost my first literary effusion, written when I was serving as a subaltern in India in 1897 was a ferocious onslaught upon him, and upon an article which he had written disparaging and deriding the British Army in some minor war. Four or five years passed before I made his acquaintance. My mother, always in agreeable contact with artistic and dramatic circles, took me to luncheon with him. I was instantly attracted by the sparkle and gaiety of his conversation, and impressed by his eating only fruit and vegetables, and drinking only water. I rallied him on the latter habit, asking "Do you really never drink any wine at all?" "I am hard enough to keep in order as it is", he replied. Perhaps he had heard of my youthful prejudice against him.

I possess a lively image of this bright, nimble, fierce, and comprehending being, Jack Frost dancing bespangled in the sunshine, which I should be very sorry to lose.

The influence of the nineties on him is strong. All the bubbling and conceit of New Movements (in capitals) took hold of him. For nine years he had been living in London under the pinch of poverty and the sharper twinges of success denied. This energetic, groping, angry man of about thirty, poor, the author of some unsuccessful novels and of some slashing criticisms with a good knowledge of music and painting, and a command of the highlights of indignation, meets in middle age Henry George, and at once joins the Fabian Society with eager enthusiasm. He speaks at hotels and street corners. He conquers his nervousness. His snuff-coloured suit, his hat turned (for some obscure economy) back to front, his black coat blending slowly into green, were gradually becoming known. Jobs slowly came in – musical criticism, dramatic criticism, political squibs and paragraphs, but it was not until 1892 that his first play *Widowers' Houses* appeared.

NARRATOR The play arose out of Shaw's first meeting with William Archer in 1885.

ARCHER I learned from himself that he was the author of several unpublished masterpieces of fiction. Construction, he owned with engaging modesty, was not his strong part, but his dialogue was incomparable. I considered myself a born conductor. So I proposed, and Mr. Shaw agreed, to a collaboration.

NARRATOR The setting was to be a hotel garden on the Rhine, and the denouement to consist of the hero proposing to the heroine, believing her to be the poor niece, instead of the rich daughter, of the slum landlord. He was to renounce the wealth as soon as he discovered who the girl was.

ARCHER All this I gravely propounded to Mr. Shaw, who listened with no less admirable gravity. Then I thought the matter had dropped for I heard no more of it for many weeks. I used to see Mr. Shaw at the British Museum, laboriously writing page after page of the most exquisitely neat shorthand at the rate of about three words a minute; but it did not occur to me that this was our play. After about six weeks he said to me:

SHAW — Look here, I've knocked off the first act of that play of ours and haven't come to the plot yet. In fact, I've forgotten the plot. You might tell me the story again.

NARRATOR — Three days later Shaw reported.

SHAW — I've written three pages of the second act and have used up all your plot, can you let me have some more to go on with?

NARRATOR — After the completion of Act II, Shaw read the first two acts to Archer, who fell asleep. Shaw concluded that he was not a playwright and pigeonholed the play. But in 1892, J. T. Grein, the manager of the Independent Theatre which had just put on Ibsen's *Ghosts* for the first time in England, began to look around for the new English drama, which Shaw said was bursting to express itself. J. T. Grein found no new drama at all.

SHAW — This was not to be endured. I had rashly taken up the case; and rather than let it collapse I manufactured the evidence.

NARRATOR — He added a third act, and the play was produced on December 9th 1892. The reception was mixed – the conventional newspapers disliking it.

THE TIMES — There can hardly be said to be a single estimable personage in the whole play.

MORNING LEADER — Revolting picture of Middle Class life.

ERA	Very disagreeable heroine . . . all the other characters in the play – the poor parlourmaid alone excepted – are as hateful as that of the heroine.
MODERN SOCIETY	He goes further than Ibsen, whose characters are a mixture of knaves and fools; whereas in *Widowers' Houses* they are all knaves.

NARRATOR But the criticism of Archer himself in *The World* rankled most.

ARCHER A set of blood-suckers. Everyone is ill-conditioned, quarrelsome, fractious, apt to behave, at a moment's notice, like a badly brought-up child.

NARRATOR Shaw's subsequent post-card to Archer read:

SHAW Here am I, who have collected slum rents weekly with these hands, and for $4\frac{1}{2}$ years been behind the scenes of the middle-class landowner, who have philandered with women of all sorts and sizes – and I am told gravely to go to nature and give up apriorising about such matters by you, you sentimental sweet lavandery recluse.

NARRATOR Archer was converted by Shaw's next play but one, *Mrs. Warren's Profession* (1893), in which a fashionably brought-up daughter discovers that the money for her upbringing has come from her mother's prostitution. But the Lord Chamberlain banned it. Shaw was outraged.

CHESTERTON Shaw found in the quarrel with the censor one of the important occasions of his life. He did not linger over loose excuses for a licence; he declared that the Censor was licentious, while he, Bernard Shaw, was clean. He did not discuss where a Censorship ought to make the drama moral. He declared that it made the drama immoral. With a fine strategic audacity he attacked the Censor quite as much for what he permitted as for what he prevented. He charged him with encouraging all plays that attracted men to vice and only stopping those which discouraged them from it.

NARRATOR But Chesterton saw another side to the dispute. An event may in itself be quite moral, he said,

CHESTERTON But it may easily be a shade too ugly for the shape of a work of art. There is nothing wrong about being sick; but if Bernard Shaw wrote a play in which all the characters expressed their dislike of animal food by vomiting on the stage, I think we should be justified in saying that the thing was outside, not the laws of morality, but the framework of civilised literature.

No-one who was alive at the time and interested in such matters will ever forget the first acting of *Arms and the Man* in April 1894. The play opens in an atmosphere of military melodrama; the dashing officer of cavalry going off to death in an attitude, the lovely heroine left in tearful rapture; the brass band, the noise of guns and the red fire. Into all this enters Bluntschli, the little sturdy crop-haired Swiss professional soldier. He tells the army-adoring heroine that she is a humbug; and she, after a moment's reflection, appears to agree with him.

NARRATOR Captain Bluntschli is fleeing, with the Serbian army, from the victorious Bulgarians. He has Just taken refuge in an indignant Raina's bedroom, by climbing in through the window, and survived an attack of inspecting officers.

BLUNTSCHLI (*Pleasantly*) You don't mind my waiting just a minute or two, do you?

RAINA (*Putting on her most genteel society manner*) Oh, not at all. Won't you sit down?

BLUNTSCHLI Thanks (*He sits on the foot of the bed*).

(*Raina walks with studied elegance to the ottoman and sits down. Unfortunately she sits on his pistol and jumps up with a shriek. Bluntschli, all nerves, shies like a frightened horse to the other side of the room.*)

BLUNTSCHLI (*irritably*) Don't frighten me like that. What is it?

RAINA Your revolver! It was staring that officer in the face all the time. What an escape.

BLUNTSCHLI (*vexed at being unnecessarily terrified*) Oh, is that all?

RAINA (*staring at him rather superciliously as she conceives a poorer and poorer opinion of him, and feels proportionately more and more at her ease*) I'm sorry I frightened you. (*She takes up the pistol and hands it to him.*) Pray take it to protect yourself against me.

BLUNTSCHLI (*Grinning wearily at the sarcasm as he takes the pistol*) No use, dear young lady: there's nothing in it. It's not loaded.

RAINA Load it by all means.

BLUNTSCHLI I've no ammunition. What use are cartridges in battle? I always carry chocolate instead; and I finished the last cake of that hours ago.

RAINA (*outraged in her most cherished ideals of manhood*) Chocolate! Do you stuff your pockets with sweets – like a schoolboy – even in the field?

BLUNTSCHLI (*grinning*) Yes: isn't it contemptible? (*Hungrily*) I wish I had some now.

RAINA Allow me. (*She sails away scornfully to the chest of drawers, and returns with the box of confectionery in her hand*) I am sorry I have eaten them all except these (*She offers him the box*)

BLUNTSCHLI (*ravenously*) You're an angel. (*He gobbles the contents*) Creams! delicious! Bless you, dear

lady! You can always tell an old soldier by the inside of his holsters and cartridge boxes. The young ones carry pistols and cartridges: the old ones, grub. Thank you. (*He hands back the box. She snatches it contemptuously from him and throws it away. He shies, as if she meant to strike him*) Ugh! Don't do things so suddenly gracious lady. It's mean to revenge yourself because I frightened you just now.

RAINA (*loftily*) Frighten me! Do you know, Sir, that though I am only a woman, I think I am at heart as brave as you.

BLUNTSCHLI I should think so. You haven't been under fire for three days as I have. I can stand two days without showing it much; but no man can stand three days. I'm as nervous as a mouse (*He sits down on the ottoman and takes his head in his hands*). Would you like to see me cry?

RAINA (*alarmed*) No.

BLUNTSCHLI If you would, all you have to do is to scold me just as if I were a little boy and you my nurse. If I were in camp now, they'd play all sorts of tricks on me.

RAINA I'm sorry. I won't scold you. You must excuse me: our soldiers are not like that.

BLUNTSCHLI Oh yes they are. There are only two sorts of soldiers: Old ones and young ones. I've served fourteen years: half of your fellows never smelt powder before. Why, how is it that you've just beaten us? Sheer ignorance of the art of war, nothing else. (*Indignantly*) I never saw anything so unprofessional.

RAINA Oh! was it unprofessional to beat you?

BLUNTSCHLI Well, come! is it professional to throw a regiment of cavalry on a battery of machine guns, with the dead certainty that if the guns go off not a horse or man will ever get within fifty yards of the fire? I couldn't believe my eyes when I saw it.

RAINA (*eagerly turning to him, as all her enthusiasm and her dreams of glory rush back to her*) Did you see the great cavalry charge? Oh, tell me about it. Describe it to me.

BLUNTSCHLI You never saw a cavalry charge, did you?

RAINA How could I?

BLUNTSCHLI Ah, perhaps not. No; of course not! Well, it's a funny sight. It's like slinging a handful of peas against a window pane: first one comes; then two or three close behind him; and then all the rest in a lump.

RAINA Yes, first one! the bravest of the brave!

BLUNTSCHLI Hm! You should see the poor devil pulling at his horse.

RAINA I don't believe the first man is a coward. I know he is a hero!

BLUNTSCHLI (*Good humouredly*) That's what you'd have said if you'd seen the first man in the charge today.

RAINA (*breathless, forgiving him everything*) Ah, I knew it! Tell me. Tell me about him.

BLUNTSCHLI He did it like an operatic tenor. A regular handsome fellow, with flashing eyes and a lovely moustache, shouting his war cry and charging like Don Quixote at the windmills. We did laugh.

RAINA You dared to laugh!

BLUNTSCHLI Yes, but when the sergeant ran up as white as a sheet, and told us they'd sent us the wrong ammunition, and that we couldn't fire a round for ten minutes, we laughed at the other side of our mouths. I never felt so sick in my life; though I've been in one or two very tight places. And I hadn't even a revolver cartridge: only chocolate. We'd no bayonets: nothing. Of course, they just cut us to bits. And there was Don Quixote flourishing like a drum major, thinking he'd done the cleverest thing ever known, whereas he ought to be court-martialled for it. Of all the fools ever let loose on a field of battle, that man must be the very maddest. He and his regiment simply committed suicide; only the pistol missed fire: that's all.

RAINA (*Deeply wounded, but steadfastly loyal to her ideals*) Indeed! Would you know him again if you saw him?

BLUNTSCHLI Shall I ever forget him!

(*She goes to the chest of drawers. She takes the portrait from its stand and brings it to him*)

RAINA That is a photograph of the gentleman – the patriot and hero – to whom I am betrothed.

BLUNTSCHLI (*recognises it with a shock*) I'm really very sorry. Yes, that's Don Quixote: not a doubt of it.

(*He stifles a laugh*) . . .

NARRATOR The actors, puzzled by the play, played it seriously on the first night. As a result *Arms and the Man* was a tremendous success. Shaw came on stage at the end. There was tremendous applause – and a solitary boo.

SHAW My dear fellow, I quite agree with you; but what are we two against so many?

NARRATOR The boo-er was Golding Bright, later famous as a theatre critic and theatre agent. Shaw and Bright subsequently met and kept up a long correspondence. But Bright remained critical:

BRIGHT His words fall meaninglessly to the ground because his ideas are expressed in insoluble terms of his own personality. "To be intelligible is to be found out", he may retort in the words of a fellow Irishman and wit, but the pertinacious presentment of himself as protagonist of each and all his works does not make for drama, but for sheer boredom and extinction.

NARRATOR The Prince of Wales saw the play and commented.

P OF W Of course he's mad.

NARRATOR Though he was to laugh so heartily at a later Shaw play, *John Bull's Other Island,* that he broke his chair. Critical reaction to Shaw's plays has always been mixed.

WEEKLY DISPATCH It would be readable and might be useful as a Fabian pamphlet.

PENNY ILLUSTRATED PAPER His propaganda – I beg pardon, his new play.

NARRATOR Golding Bright was more puzzled about the plays.

BRIGHT *Mrs. Warren's Profession,* though dealing with a revolting subject, is a work of such amazing vigour and extraordinary power as almost to stupefy the coolest-headed. . . . There remains Candida, and, for the sake of its purity and strength, one would willingly forget the remaining works – good, bad and indifferent. It is because Mr. Shaw has, for once, not been ashamed to figure as a man of sentiment that he has succeeded in writing a really beautiful play where he failed before through excess of brainishness.

NARRATOR Winston Churchill summed up the layman's dilemma.

CHURCHILL The plays were startling enough on their first appearance. Ibsen had broken the "well-made play" by making it better than ever: Mr. Shaw broke it by not "making" it at all. He was once told that Sir James Barrie had completely worked out the plot of "Shall we Join the Ladies" before he began to write it. Mr. Shaw was scandalised. "Fancy knowing how a play is to end before you begin it! When *I* start a play I haven't the slightest idea what is going to happen." His other main innovation was to depend for his drama not on the interplay of character and character, or of character and circumstance, but on that of argument and argument. His ideas become personages, and fight among themselves, sometimes with intense dramatic effect, and sometimes not. His human beings, with a few exceptions, are there for what they are to say, not for what they are to be or do. Yet they live.

NARRATOR Shaw had a simple theory about why he appeared original.

SHAW I found that the surest way to produce an effect of daring innovation and originality was to revive the ancient attraction of long speeches; to stick closely to the methods of Moliere; and to lift characters bodily out of the pages of Charles Dickens.

NARRATOR — "His prose is very simple. At least it sounds very simple, which is the important thing in the theatre. Yet its athleticism and vitality are of a quality unique in theatre," wrote Eric Bentley. The following episode from Pygmalion illustrates Shaw's skill in dialogue and a notorious example of his power to shock his audiences.

(*Eliza, who is exquisitely dressed, produces an impression of such remarkable distinction and beauty as she enters that they all rise, quite fluttered. Guided by Higgins's signals, she comes to Mrs. Higgins with studied grace.*)

LIZA — (*Speaking with pedantic correctness of pronunciation and great beauty of tone*) How do you do, Mrs. Higgins? (*She gasps slightly in making sure of the H in Higgins, but is quite successful*) Mr. Higgins told me I might come.

MRS. HIGGINS — (*cordially*) Quite right: I'm very glad indeed to see you.

PICKERING — How do you do, Miss Doolittle?

LIZA — (*Shaking hands with him*) Colonel Pickering, is it not?

MRS. EYNSFORD HILL — I feel sure we have met before, Miss Doolittle. I remember your eyes.

LIZA — How do you do?

MRS. EYNSFORD HILL — My daughter Clara.

LIZA — How do you do?

FREDDY — I've certainly had the pleasure.

MRS. EYNSFORD HILL — My son Freddy.

LIZA How do you do?

(*Freddy bows and sits down in the Elizabethan chair, infatuated.*)

(*A long and painful pause ensues*)

MRS. HIGGINS (*at last, conversationally*) Will it rain, do you think?

LIZA The shallow depression in the west of these islands is likely to move in an easterly direction. There are no indications of any great change in the barometrical situation.

FREDDY Ha! Ha! how awfully funny!

LIZA What is wrong with that, young man. I bet I got it right.

FREDDY Killing!

MRS. EYNSFORD HILL I'm sure I hope it won't turn cold. There's so much influenza about. It runs right through our whole family regularly every spring.

LIZA (*darkly*) My aunt died of influenza, so they said.

MRS. EYNSFORD HILL (*clicks her tongue sympathetically*)!

LIZA (*In the same tragic tone*) But it's my belief they done the old woman in.

MRS. HIGGINS (*puzzled*) Done her in?

LIZA Y-e-e-e-es, Lord love you! Why should she die of influenza? She come through diphtheria right enough the year before. I saw her with my own eyes. Fairly blue with it, she was. They all thought she was dead; but my father he kept ladling gin down her throat 'til she came to so sudden that she bit the bowl off the spoon.

MRS. EYNSFORD HILL (*startled*) Dear me!

LIZA (*Piling up the indictment*) What call would a woman with that strength in her have to die of influenza? What became of her new straw hat that should have come to me? Somebody pinched it; and what I say is, them as pinched it done her in.

MRS. EYNSFORD HILL What does doing her in mean?

HIGGINS (*hastily*) Oh, that's the new small talk. To do a person in means to kill them.

MRS. EYNSFORD HILL You surely don't believe your aunt was killed?

LIZA Do I not! Them she lived with would have killed her for a hat-pin, let alone a hat.

MRS. EYNSFORD HILL But it can't have been right for your father to pour spirits down her throat like that. It might have killed her.

LIZA Not her. Gin was mother's milk to her. Besides he'd poured so much down his own throat that he knew the good of it.

MRS. EYNSFORD HILL Do you mean that he drank?

LIZA Drank! My word! Something chronic.

MRS. EYNSFORD HILL How dreadful for you.

LIZA Not a bit. It never did him no harm what I could see. But then he did not keep it up regular. (*Cheerfully*) On the burst, as you might say, from time to time. And always more agreeable when he had a drop in. When he was out of work, my mother used to give him fourpence and tell him to go out and not come back until he'd drunk himself cheerful and loving-like. There's lots of women has to make their husbands drink to make them fit to live with. (*Now quite at her ease*) You see, it's like this. If a man has a bit of a conscience, it always takes him when he's sober; and then makes him low-spirited. A drop of booze just takes that off and makes him happy (*To Freddy, who is in convulsions of suppressed laughter*) Here! What are you sniggering at?

FREDDY — The new small talk. You do it so awfully well.

LIZA — If I was doing it proper, what was you laughing at? (*To Higgins*) Have I said anything I oughtn't?

MRS. HIGGINS — (*interposing*) Not at all, Miss Doolittle.

LIZA — Well, that's a mercy, anyhow. (*Expansively*) What I always say is . . .

HIGGINS — (*rising and looking at his watch*) Ahem!

LIZA — (*looking round at him and taking the hint*) Well I must go. (*They all rise. Freddy goes to the door*) So pleased to have met you. Goodbye. (*She shakes hands with Mrs. Higgins*).

MRS. HIGGINS — Goodbye.

LIZA — Goodbye, Colonel Pickering.

PICKERING — Goodbye, Miss Doolittle. (*They shake hands*)

LIZA — (*nodding to the others*) Goodbye all.

FREDDY (*opening the door for her*) Are you walking across the Park, Miss Doolittle? If so . . .

LIZA (*with perfectly elegant diction*) Walk! Not bloody likely! (*Sensation*) I am going in a taxi (*She goes out*)

NARRATOR W. H. Auden has written:

AUDEN All his life Shaw has been devoted to music (he was probably the best music critic who ever lived) and, as he tells us, it was from Mozart's *Don Giovanni* that he learned "how to write seriously without being dull"; and this devotion is, perhaps, the clue to his work. For all his theatre about propaganda, his writing has an effect nearer to that of music than any of the so-called pure writers.

NARRATOR Shaw was not always patient with anyone who praised the simplicity of his style.

SHAW It was very much as If I had told him the house was on fire, and he had said, "How admirably monosyllabic!"

NARRATOR Looking back on his earlier plays, Shaw found them flimsy compared with his later plays. As he grew older, Shaw's philosophy grew naturally more profound. He frequently lectured on religious topics, and his most admired plays have dealt with religious characters and themes. His philosophy can briefly be called a reaction against Darwin.

SHAW In the middle of the last century all the mind, conscience, and intelligence of the best part of mankind was in revolt against the old-fashioned conception of God, and yet at the same time finding itself intellectually unable to get away from the conception of God the Designer. They were in a dilemma. There must be what they called God, and yet they could not make him responsible for the good in the world without making him also responsible for the evil, because they never questioned one thing about him: that, being the designer of the Universe, he must be necessarily omnipotent. This being the situation, is it not clear that if at that time any man had risen up and said, "All this wonderful adaptation of means to end, all this design which seems to imply a designer, is an illusion; it may have all come about by the operation of what we call blind chance", the most intelligent and best part of the human race without stopping to criticise his argument very closely, would spring at that man and take him to their arms as a moral saviour, saying, "You have lifted from our minds this horrible conception that the force that is governing us all and is managing the whole world is hideous, criminal, cruel?" That is exactly what happened when Charles Darwin appeared and the reason why he had such an enormous success that the religion of the last half of the nineteenth century became Darwinian.

Earlier, Lamarck, a Frenchman, gave an illustration of the process of evolution. He said that the reason the giraffe had a long neck is that this creature wanted to feed on the soft herbiage on the top of tall trees, and by dint of generations of giraffes stretching their necks, they gradually made their necks longer, until they could reach the requisite height. Now that means that the giraffe got a long neck because it wanted a long neck.

But Darwin said, in effect, "I can explain the giraffe's long neck without implying the slightest purpose or will. Supposing a few giraffes happened to have necks a little longer than the others, they would be able to reach vegetation, while their less fortunate fellows starved. Consequently the longer-necked giraffes would survive while the others perished and produce a race of giraffes with necks a little longer, and this without any purpose or design.

Samuel Butler declared with penetrating accuracy that Darwin had "banished mind from the Universe."

NARRATOR After the First World War Shaw said:

SHAW At the present moment one half of Europe, having knocked the other half down, is trying to kick it to death, and may succeed: a procedure which is logically sound Neo-Darwinism.

The Neo-Darwinists held that there is no such thing as self-control. What *is* self-control? It is nothing but a highly developed vital sense, dominating and regulating the mere appetites. To overlook the very existence of the supreme sense; to miss the obvious inference that it is this quality that distinguishes the fittest to survive . . . all this, which the Neo-Darwinians did in the name of Natural Selection, showed the the most pitiable want of mastery of their own subject.

NARRATOR So the only thing left to postulate is a God who does design – but could design better. A newspaper headline ran

HEADLINE "God makes mistakes" – Bernard Shaw.

SHAW We may regard the typhoid bacillus as one of the failures of the life force that we call God, but that same force is trying through our brains to discover some method of destroying that malign influence. If you get that conception, you will be able to give an answer to those people who ask for an explanation of the origin of evil. Evil things are things that are made with the object of their doing good, but turn out wrong and have to be destroyed.

We are all experiments in the direction of making God. What God is doing is making himself, getting from being a mere powerless will or force. This force has implanted into our minds the ideal of God. We are not very successful attempts at God so far, but I believe that if we can drive into the heads of men the full consciousness of moral responsibility that comes to men with the knowledge that there never can be a God unless we make him . . . we can work towards that ideal until we get to be supermen, and then super-supermen, and then a world of organisms which have achieved and realised God.

NARRATOR In some unprepared remarks to the National Liberal Club, Shaw spoke of the ideal of the individual

SHAW What is the ideal of a Gentleman? He says in effect: "I want to be a cultured human being; I want to live in the fullest sense; I require a generous subsistence for that; and I expect my country to organise itself in such a way as to secure me that." Also the real gentleman says – and here is where the real gentleman parts company with the sham gentleman, of whom we have so many: "In return for that I am willing to give my country the best service of which I am capable; absolutely the best. My ideal shall be also that, no matter how much I have demanded from my country, or how much my country has given me, I hope, and I shall strive, to give my Country in return more than it has given to me; so that when I die my country shall be richer for my life.

NARRATOR Which explains Shaw's devotion to practical political causes (his membership of the St. Pancras Borough Council for example) long after he had become a popular playwright.

SHAW — The only real tragedy in life is the being used by personally minded men for purposes which you recognise to be base.

NARRATOR — Shaw's faith in humanity was shaken by the events of the First World War.

SHAW — Neo-Darwinism in politics had produced a European catastrophe of a magnitude so appalling, and a scope so unpredictable, that as I write these lines in 1920, it is still far from certain whether our civilisation will survive it. The circumstances of this catastrophe, the boyish cinema-fed romaticism which made it possible to impose it on the people as a crusade, and especially the ignorance and errors of the victors of Western Europe when its violent phase had passed and the time for reconstruction arrived, confirmed a doubt which has grown steadily in my mind during my forty years in public work as a socialist: namely, whether the human animal, as he exists at present, is capable of solving the social problems raised by his own aggregation, or, as he calls it, his civilisation.

NARRATOR — Just as he had attacked Darwinism, so he turned his attack on the scientists. Not because the scientific approach was wrong: but because scientific solutions and methods were too readily accepted. He became an opponent of vivisection, because it was pointless, he said, and wasteful. He distrusted all scientific conclusions. When told that the sun was 92,000,000 miles away he replied.

SHAW — Nonsense! Look at it!

NARRATOR — And worked out that it was 37 miles off. His approach has been described as "a romantic's plea for the evidence of the senses". He looked for a moral, not a scientific authority.

SHAW The Church has failed infamously. I can hardly imagine how it has the face to exist after its recreancy during the War. The Church of England is only a Society of gentlemen amateurs, half of them pretending to be properly trained and disciplined priests, and the other half pretending to be breezy public schoolboys with no parsonic nonsense about them.

NARRATOR Shaw's pamphlet "Commonsense About the War" made him a much hated figure. H. G. Wells described him as:

H. G. WELLS An idiot child laughing in a hospital.

NARRATOR His fellow playwright, Henry Arthur Jones, after leading an attack on him which culminated in his expulsion from the Dramatists' Club, called him

H. A. JONES A freakish homunculus germinated outside lawful procreation.

NARRATOR But Shaw escaped serious trouble.

SHAW I suppose that I escape lynching solely because people treat everything I say as a huge joke; the point being that if a solitary word I uttered were taken seriously the whole social order would be endangered. Well, there's something in that. If people didn't laugh at me they couldn't endure me. As an ordinary human being I am frankly impossible; even as a variety turn I am only just bearable. My mental and moral superiority are insufferable. No chink can be observed by the naked eye in my armour. Such a preposterous personification of repulsive virtues is intolerable. So my fellow-citizens stuff their fingers in their ears and drown my words in senseless cackle.

NARRATOR But Winston Churchill pressed the point further.

CHURCHILL When nations are fighting for life, when the Palace in which the jester dwells not uncomfortably is itself assailed, and everyone from Prince to Groom is fighting on the battlements, the jester's jokes echo only through deserted halls, and his witticisms and commendations, distributed evenly though between friend and foe, jar the ears of hurrying messengers, of mourning women and wounded men. The titter ill accords with the tocsin or the motley with the bandages.

NARRATOR He has a less stern, but more damaging, conclusion.

CHURCHILL He has laughed his sparkling way through life, exploding by his own acts or words every argument he has ever used on either side of any question, teasing and bewildering every public he has addressed, and involving in his own mockery every cause he had ever championed. The world has long watched with tolerance and amusement the nimble antics and gyrations of this unique and double-headed chameleon, while all the time the creature was eager to be taken seriously.

NARRATOR Father Keegan in John Bull's Other Island.

KEEGAN In my dreams heaven is a country where the State is the Church and the Church the People: three in one and one in three. It is a Commonwealth in which work is play and play is life: three in one and one in three. It is a temple in which the priest is a worshipper and the worshipper is worshipped: three in one and one in three. It is a god-head in which all life is human and all humanity divine: three in

one and one in three. It is, in short, the dream of a madman.

SHAW Whether it be that I was born mad or a little too sane, my kingdom was not of this world: I was at home only in the realm of my imagination, and at ease only with the mighty dead.

NARRATOR He was not unlike St. Joan a figure who, in her hopeless struggle but her indomitable spirit, may be allowed to speak for Shaw himself.

JOAN O God that madest this beautiful earth, when will it be ready to receive Thy Saints. How long, O Lord, how long?

THE END